THE RIVER LOIRE CYCLE ROUTE

THE RIVER LOIRE CYCLE ROUTE

FROM THE SOURCE IN THE MASSIF CENTRAL TO THE ATLANTIC COAST

by Mike Wells

JUNIPER HOUSE, MURLEY MOSS,
OXENHOLME ROAD, KENDAL, CUMBRIA LA9 7RL
www.cicerone.co.uk

© Mike Wells 2022
Third edition 2022
ISBN: 978 1 78631 083 5
First edition 2013
Second edition 2017

Printed in China on responsibly sourced paper on behalf of Latitude Press Ltd
A catalogue record for this book is available from the British Library.
All photographs are by the author unless otherwise stated.

Route mapping by Lovell Johns www.lovelljohns.com
Contains OpenStreetMap.org data © OpenStreetMap
contributors, CC-BY-SA. NASA relief data courtesy of ESRI

Updates to this guide

While every effort is made by our authors to ensure the accuracy of guidebooks as they go to print, changes can occur during the lifetime of an edition, and it is possible that the COVID pandemic may give rise to more changes to routes or facilities than would usually be expected. Any updates that we know of for this guide will be on the Cicerone website (www.cicerone.co.uk/1083/updates), so please check before planning your trip. We also advise that you check information about such things as transport, accommodation and shops locally. Even rights of way can be altered over time.

The route maps in this guide are derived from publicly-available data, databases and crowd-sourced data. As such they have not been through the detailed checking procedures that would generally be applied to a published map from an official mapping agency, although naturally we have reviewed them closely in the light of local knowledge as part of the preparation of this guide.

We are always grateful for information about any discrepancies between a guidebook and the facts on the ground, sent by email to updates@cicerone.co.uk or by post to Cicerone, Juniper House, Murley Moss, Oxenholme Road, Kendal, LA9 7RL.

Front cover: Amboise château was the royal palace in the 15th and 16th century

CONTENTS

Notre-Dame basilica towers over La Vieux Bourg hamlet (Stage 24)

PREFACE TO THIS EDITION

In addition to a few minor changes which reflect road management schemes including new roundabouts, cycle lanes and changed signposting, this guide includes a number of significant route changes, mostly on the upper Loire before Digoin. At Le-Puy-en Velay (Stage 2) increased use is made of voie verte V73 along the trackbed of an old railway, while between Montrond-les-Bains and Digoin (Stages 5–7), the route now uses the newly waymarked 'Véloire' route (V71) which includes sections along the towpath of the canal de Roanne à Digoin and the trackbed of another old railway. The French authorities intend to extend V71 south from Montrond to connect with V73 in Lavoûte north of Le Puy (Stage 3). Although there is not yet a definite route, the route descriptions have been adapted to take these proposals into account.

There have been fewer route changes to EuroVelo 6 and La Loire à Vélo (Stages 8–26). A fully waymarked alternative route is now used to visit Angers via the Trélazé slate quarries (Stage 22), while between Oudon and Mauves-sur-Loire (Stage 25) danger of rockfalls from a riverside cliff face has been circumvented by diverting the route along the opposite side of the river. From Paimbœuf–St Brevin-les-Pins (Stage 26) the previous provisional road route has been replaced by a new cycle track alongside the Loire estuary.

Increasing popularity with cyclists has led to an increase in the number of *gîtes d'étape* (cheap overnight accommodation in shared rooms) on or close to the route and these are listed in an expanded Appendix C. The regulations and provision for the carriage of cycles by train have also changed. Eurostar now charge differential prices between fully assembled bikes (two per train) and disassembled ones (four per train). In France, only a few TGV trains serving the Rhone valley have cycle spaces, making it sometimes necessary to use TER regional express trains from Paris Bercy to Lyon and Lyon to Valence with increased journey times.

ROUTE SUMMARY TABLE

Stage	Start	Finish	Distance (km)	Waymarking	Page
1	Gerbier de Jonc	Goudet	50	Vivez la Loire Sauvage	47
2	Goudet	Le Puy-en-Velay	33	Vivez la Loire Sauvage	53
3	Le Puy-en-Velay	Retournac	37	Vivez la Loire Sauvage	58
4	Retournac	Aurec-sur-Loire	30	Vivez la Loire Sauvage	64
5	Aurec-sur-Loire	Feurs	58.5	Véloire V71 (planned)	69
6	Feurs	Roanne	62.5	Véloire V71	79
7	Roanne	Digoin	58	Véloire V71	88
8	Digoin	Bourbon-Lancy	31	EV6	95
9	Bourbon-Lancy	Decize	46	EV6	100
10	Decize	Nevers (Verville)	34	EV6	105
11	Nevers (Verville)	La Charité-sur-Loire	40	EV6 then Loire à Vélo	110
12	La Charité-sur-Loire	Sancerre (St Thibault)	24	Loire à Vélo	116
13	Sancerre (St Thibault)	Briare	43	Loire à Vélo	121
14	Briare	Sully-sur-Loire	40.5	Loire à Vélo	128
15	Sully-sur-Loire	Orléans	50.5	Loire à Vélo	135
16	Orléans	Beaugency	28	Loire à Vélo	144
17	Beaugency	Blois	34.5	Loire à Vélo	150
18	Blois	Amboise	42	Loire à Vélo	159
19	Amboise	Tours	27	Loire à Vélo	168
20	Tours	Bréhémont	35	Loire à Vélo	175
21	Bréhémont	Saumur	47.5	Loire à Vélo	181
22	Saumur	Angers (Les Ponts-de-Cé)	50	Loire à Vélo	190
23	Angers (Les Ponts-de-Cé)	Montjean-sur-Loire	36.5	Loire à Vélo	202
24	Montjean-sur-Loire	Ancenis	28.5	Loire à Vélo	209
25	Ancenis	Nantes	39	Loire à Vélo	214
26	Nantes	St Brevin-les-Pins	55	Loire à Vélo	222
		Total distance	**1061**		

Canal Latéral à la Loire at Chavanne (Stage 8)

INTRODUCTION

To best discover a country you need to travel to its very heart and do so in a way that exposes you to the life going on around you. The river Loire passes through the heart of France and there is no better way of experiencing life in this great country than by mounting your bicycle and following this river as it flows from the volcanic landscape of the Massif Central to the Atlantic Ocean. Its length of 1020km makes it the longest river in France. Here you will find a gentler and slower pace of life than in the great cities of Paris, Lyon or Marseille; and although there is some industry, it is less evident in the Loire Valley than alongside France's other major rivers.

Rather, this is a land of agriculture and vineyards. The Beauce, north of Orléans, has some of the most fertile arable farmland in the country, while the rolling hills of the Auvergne and Burgundy produce high-quality meat and dairy products. The plains of Anjou grow much of the fruit and vegetables found in the markets and restaurants of Paris, often consumed with wines from premier Loire wine-growing appellations like Muscadet, Pouilly Fumé, Sancerre and Vouvray. All this great food and drink can also be found in restaurants along the route.

The Loire is known to the French as the 'Royal River' – a name it gets

Most French towns have markets like this one in Vorey (Stage 3)

Château de Chaumont was the home of Catherine de Medici, Henri II's queen (Stage 18)

from the Loire Valley's long association with the kings of France after successive monarchs developed a series of ever more spectacular *châteaux* between the 15th and 17th centuries. Blois and Amboise were great palaces where the royal court resided to escape political turmoil in Paris. Chambord was a glorious hunting lodge, from where the king would spend long days hunting in the forests of the Sologne, while Chenonceau was home first for a royal mistress and later a widowed queen. The preference of the royal family for life along the Loire stimulated other members of the court to build their own châteaux in the area, with over 50 nowadays recognised as heritage sites by UNESCO. Although most of these were sequestered, damaged and looted during the French Revolution,

20th-century restoration has breathed new life into them and many can now be visited.

In addition to secular buildings, the Loire Valley holds a strong religious presence. Le Puy-en-Velay, with a church and iron Madonna each perched on top of volcanic spires and a great basalt cathedral, is a popular starting point for the pilgrimage route to Santiago in Spain. Tours has both a great cathedral that took so long to build it is in three different styles (Romanesque, Gothic and Renaissance) and also a basilica built to house the tomb of French patron saint St Martin, a Roman soldier who became an early bishop of Tours. Other French saints encountered include St Benedict (founder of the Benedictine order), buried at Fleury Abbey in St Benoît, and Ste Bernadette

Château de Montsoreau (Stage 21)

of Lourdes whose preserved body is on display in Nevers. Ste Jeanne d'Arc, a French national heroine who lifted the siege of Orléans and turned the tide of the Hundred Years' War in favour of France, is widely commemorated, particularly in Orléans itself. Furthermore, the little village of Germigny-des-Prés has a church from the time of Charlemagne (AD806) that claims to be the oldest in France.

These châteaux, cathedrals, monasteries, churches and the countryside between them are linked by the Loire Cycle Route. This 1061km route starts beside the river's source on the slopes of the volcanic plug of Gerbier de Jonc and follows a waymarked route, Vivez la Loire Sauvage, through a series of gorges downhill between the wooded volcanic cones and basalt plateaux of the Auvergne. After leaving the mountains it passes the Charolais hills and at Digoin joins EuroVelo route EV6, which itself joins a French national cycle trail, La Loire à Vélo, near Nevers. This is followed, mostly on level, dedicated cycle tracks, through Orléans, Tours, Angers and Nantes to reach the Atlantic opposite the shipbuilding town of St Nazaire. This is the most popular cycle route in France, followed by thousands of cyclists every year. French regional and département governments have invested heavily in infrastructure with well-defined waymarking, asphalt-surfaced tracks, dedicated bridges over rivers and underpasses beneath roads along the route. Almost every town and many large villages have tourist offices that can point you in the direction of (and often book for you) overnight accommodation that varies from five-star hotels to village gîtes d'étape.

BACKGROUND

The Loire passes through the heart of France. Modern France, the Fifth French Republic, is the current manifestation of a great colonial nation that developed out of Charlemagne's eighth-century Frankish kingdom, eventually spreading its power throughout Europe and beyond.

Roman France

Before the arrival of the Romans in the first century BC, central France was inhabited by Iron Age Celtic tribes like the Gauls. The Romans involved local tribal leaders in government and control of the territory. With improvements in the standard of living, the conquered tribes soon became thoroughly Romanised and Gallic settlements became Romano-Gallic towns. During the fourth century AD the Romans came under increasing pressure from Germanic tribes from the east, and by AD401 had withdrawn their legions from central France and the Loire Valley.

The Franks and the foundation of France

After the Romans left there followed a period of tribal settlement. The

Franks were a tribe that settled in northern France. From AD496, when Clovis I became their king and established a capital in Paris, the Frankish kingdom expanded by absorbing neighbouring states. Charlemagne (a Frank, AD768–814) temporarily united much of western Europe, only for his Carolingian empire to be split in 843, after which the Franks became the dominant regional force. The kingdom of France grew by defeating and absorbing neighbouring duchies. In the Loire basin, Anjou was captured in 1214 and Auvergne was absorbed in 1271.

The Hundred Years' War

One particular neighbour proved hard to defeat. Ever since Vikings settled in Normandy and around the mouth of the Loire in the ninth century, there had been a threat from the west. The Vikings became the Normans, and when in 1066 they annexed England, their power base became larger. For nearly 400 years the Norman kings of England and their Plantagenet successors sought to consolidate and expand their territory in France. The main confrontation was the Hundred Years' War (1337–1453) fought between France and an alliance of England and

Rue Jeanne d'Arc leads to Orléans cathedral (Stage 15)

Burgundy. For many years the English and Burgundians had the upper hand, capturing large areas of France. The turning point came in 1429 when a French force led by a 17-year-old girl, Jeanne d'Arc (Joan of Arc), succeeded in lifting the siege of Orléans. By 1453 the English had been driven almost completely out of France, consolidating the French monarchy as the dominant force in the region. When Burgundy (1477) and Brittany (1532) were absorbed, the French king controlled the entire Loire basin.

The Wars of Religion and the Huguenots

The Protestant Reformation spread to France from Germany and Switzerland in the early 16th century and rapidly took hold, driven by a widespread perception of corruption among Catholic clergy. By mid-century many towns had substantial numbers of Protestant worshippers, known as Huguenots. This sparked a violent reaction from devout Catholics led by the Duc de Guise, and between 1562 and 1598 France was convulsed by a series of ferocious wars between religious factions. It is estimated that between two million and four million people died as a result of war, famine and disease. The wars were ended by the Edict of Nantes, which granted substantial rights and freedoms to Protestants. However, this was not the end of the dispute. Continued pressure from Catholic circles gradually reduced these freedoms and in 1685 Louis XIV revoked the Edict. Thankfully this did not provoke renewed fighting, many Huguenots choosing to avoid persecution by emigrating to Protestant countries (particularly Switzerland, Britain and the Netherlands), but it did have a very damaging effect on the national economy. Many of the towns passed in the Loire Valley suffered during these wars.

The age of the Kings

For 250 years from 1434, when Charles VII seized the château of Amboise (Stage 18), a succession of kings either lived in or spent a lot of time in their royal residences along the Loire and its nearby tributaries. Amboise became a favoured palace and an escape from the unhealthy climate and political intrigues of Paris for Louis XI (1461–1483) and Charles VIII (1483–1498), who rebuilt the château. Louis XII (1498–1515) ruled from Blois (Stage 17), where he had built the front part of the château. His successor François I (1515–1547) greatly enlarged Blois, although he preferred Amboise, which became his principal royal palace. François also commissioned the totally over-the-top Chambord (Stage 17) as a hunting lodge on the edge of the Sologne. Despite taking 28 years and needing 1800 men to build it, Chambord was used for less than seven weeks before being abandoned as impractical, following which it remained unfurnished and unused for 80 years. After François's son Henri II died his

The Duchess of Angoulême column in St Florent-le-Vieil commemorates 1000 victims of the French Revolution (Stage 24)

widow ruled from Chenonceaux as regent for underage François II. When Henri III (1574–1589) was driven from Paris by the Wars of Religion he chose to rule from Blois, as did Henri IV (1589–1610). Louis XIII (1610–1643) returned the court permanently to Paris and gave all the royal châteaux in the Loire Valley to his brother, Gaston d'Orléans, who started to restore Chambord. This restoration was continued by the keen huntsman Louis XIV (1643–1715), who furnished the château only to abandon it again in 1685.

The French Revolution

The *ancien régime* French kingdom ended in a period of violent revolution (1789–1799). The monarchy was swept away and privileges enjoyed by the nobility and clergy removed. Monasteries and religious institutions were closed while palaces and castles were expropriated by the state. Many were demolished but some survived, often serving as barracks or prisons. In place of the monarchy a secular republic was established. The revolutionary mantra of *liberté, égalité, fraternité* is still the motto of modern-day France. Chaos followed the Revolution and a Reign of Terror resulted in an estimated 40,000 deaths, including those of King Louis XVI and his wife Marie Antoinette. The west of France (Pays de Loire, Brittany and the Vendée), where resistance to the Revolution was greatest, saw the highest number of executions outside of Paris. A coup in 1799 led to military leader Napoleon Bonaparte taking control.

Napoleon Bonaparte

Despite ruling France for only 16 years, Napoleon (1769–1821) had a greater influence on the political and legal structures of the country than any other person. He made peace with the Catholic Church and allowed many exiled aristocrats to return, albeit with limited powers. In 1804 he declared himself Emperor of France and started a series of military campaigns that saw the French briefly gain control of much of western and central Europe. Perhaps the longest lasting Napoleonic reform was the Code Napoléon – a civil legal code that was adopted throughout the conquered territories and remains today at the heart of the European legal system. When Napoleon was defeated in 1815 by the combined forces of Britain and Prussia, he was replaced as head of state by a restoration of the monarchy under Louis XVIII, brother of Louis XVI.

French industrialisation

During the 19th century the French economy grew strongly, based on coal, iron and steel, and heavy engineering. In the Loire basin, St Étienne (close to Stage 5) developed as a major coal mining centre while the ironworks at Fourchambault (Stage 11) became the main producer of rails and girders for the expanding French railway and canal systems. A large overseas empire was created, mostly in Africa, and foreign trade saw Nantes (Stage 25) develop as the main port city on France's Atlantic coast, with industry built around imported products like sugar and tobacco. More infamously, Nantes was the French centre of the triangular slave trade, supplying ships that took 550,000 slaves from Africa to the Americas. Larger ships were unable to reach Nantes, leading to the development of the port city of St Nazaire (Stage 26) right at the river mouth; this became (and still is) an important shipbuilding centre.

Twentieth-century France

Despite being on the winning side, the French economy was devastated by the First World War and the depression of the 1930s. Invasion by Germany in the Second World War saw the French army retreat south across the Loire. Almost all Loire bridges were destroyed, either by the retreating army or by German bombing which also damaged many riverside towns – Gien (Stage 14) being particularly badly hit. Surrender saw France temporarily partitioned, with all of southern France becoming part of Vichy – a nominally independent state that was in reality a puppet government controlled by the Germans. In St Nazaire the occupying Germans built an impregnable submarine pen that was so vigorously defended that the city was the last in France to be liberated.

After the war, France was one of the original signatories to the Treaty of Rome (1957), which established the European Economic Community (EEC) and led to the European Union (EU). Economic growth was strong and the French economy prospered. Political dissent, particularly over colonial policy, led to a new constitution and the establishment of the Fifth Republic under Charles de Gaulle in 1958. Subsequent withdrawal from overseas colonies has led to substantial immigration into metropolitan France from ex-colonies, creating the most ethnically diverse population in Europe. Since the 1970s old heavy industry has almost completely disappeared and been replaced with high-tech industry and employment in the service sector.

Shipping on the river

The Loire is only properly navigable below its junction with the Maine near Angers (Stage 23). Above here the river is classed as *sauvage*: a wild river with shifting sandbanks, rapids at high water-flow and shallows when the flow is low with no locks or cuts to avoid them. In the past, before railways and roads provided a viable alternative, barges floating downstream took merchandise (mostly coal from St Étienne) from St Rambert (Stage 5). As river conditions prevented any upstream navigation, these were one-way trips with the barges being broken up at the end of the voyage. Bi-directional trade was possible up to Roanne (Stage 6) only when river conditions were favourable, but became possible year-round when canals that ran parallel with the river opened at the beginning of the 19th century. Small pleasure craft can still reach Roanne by a mixture of

Flat-bottomed barges like this reconstruction at La Charité-sur-Loire (Stage 11) once carried goods downstream

The volcanic plug of Mt Gerbier de Jonc (1551m) rises above the Loire source (Stage 1)

canal and river, but the Villerest dam (built 1984) prevents them going any further. There is no commercial shipping on the river nowadays, although enthusiasts have restored many old wooden Loire barges, some of which are used for commercial fishing but most for leisure pursuits.

The 1061km Loire Cycle Route starts in the Massif Central mountains of central France, then heads north to Orléans (only 100km south of Paris) before turning west to reach the Atlantic at St Nazaire. En route it passes through the French regions of Auvergne-Rhône-Alpes, Bourgogne-Franche-Comté, Centre-Val de Loire, and Pays de la Loire.

Our route (Stage 1) starts at the Loire source on the slopes of Mont Gerbier de Jonc in the Monts du Vivarais, a northern extension of the Cévennes range. From here the river is followed downhill, threading its way through a series of gorges between the *puys* (volcanic cones), crater lakes and basalt plateaux of the Massif Central before following a *voie verte* (rural cycle track) along an old railway line to reach the pilgrimage city of Le Puy-en-Velay (Stage 2). The volcanic landscape continues (Stage 3–4) with the route climbing in and out of the gorges and crossing more basalt plateaux. After Aurec the route crosses the edge of the Monts de Forez (Stage 5) before descending into the Forez basin. A final forested ridge is encountered, an outlier of the Monts de Beaujolais (Stage 6), before the route reaches Roanne, the end of the mountains and the beginning of navigation in the Loire Valley.

Canal towpaths and another voie verte are followed (Stage 7) past the Charolais hills with pastures full of eponymous cream-coloured cattle. At Digoin the route joins the towpath of the canal Latéral à la Loire, which is followed (Stage 8) most of the way to Bourbon-Lancy. Between here and Decize (Stage 9) there is no dedicated cycle way, so quiet roads are followed through gently rolling hills. After Decize the canal is regained and is followed (Stages 10–13), with a few deviations, all the way to Briare, passing opposite the city of Nevers and below the hilltop wine town of Sancerre. Beyond Briare, the Loire, which has so far flowed north, turns to a north-westerly direction, looping

round the Sologne (Stages 14–15), a huge area of forest and lakes that was very popular with French royalty and nobility for the pursuit of hunting. The city of Orléans, the most northerly point reached, was the ancient capital of France and is closely linked with the story of Jeanne d'Arc.

Downstream from Orléans, the Loire is known as the 'Royal River', so called because of the large number of royal châteaux in the area built by a succession of monarchs from the 14th–18th centuries. Between Orléans and Blois (Stages 16–17) the route first skirts the fertile Beauce plain, north of the Loire, then passes near the spectacular Château de Chambord in the Forêt de Boulogne. Blois and Amboise (Stages 18–19) both have large city-centre royal châteaux, while the smaller château at Chaumont hosts

Part of the route follows the canal Latéral à la Loire (Stages 8 and 10)

The Loire Gorges natural park seen from Chambles (Stage 5)

an annual garden festival. The river is now flowing between low chalk and limestone cliffs, into which many caves have been cut to extract building stone. These have a variety of uses nowadays, including wine cellars and mushroom farms. The basilica in Tours is the burial place of France's patron saint, St Martin, a Roman soldier who converted to Christianity and became bishop of Tours.

Stage 20 leaves the Loire briefly, following its Cher tributary past the châteaux at Villandry with an immaculately kept 100 hectares of formal gardens, and Ussé, inspiration for the story of Sleeping Beauty. There are more riverside cliffs, with the route going underground through the caves of a troglodyte village, and hillside vineyards before Saumur (Stage 21). Entering Anjou, heartland

of Norman-English France during the Hundred Years' War, an excursion can be made to visit its capital, Angers (Stage 22). Stages 23–25 follow the river through the Vendée – an area that provided the greatest level of resistance during the French Revolution – and the Muscadet wine region to reach Nantes, a city that grew rich on profits from the African slave trade. Finally the generally flat coastal plain of Loire-Atlantique is crossed (Stage 26) to reach St Brevin-les-Pins, opposite the shipbuilding town of St Nazaire.

NATURAL ENVIRONMENT

Physical geography

The Massif Central mountains are the oldest in France, formed mostly of gneiss and metamorphic schists. When the African and European tectonic plates collided approximately 30 million years ago, pushing up the Alps and raising the eastern edge of the Massif Central, they triggered a series of eruptions that formed a chain of volcanoes in the eastern and central parts of the range. Subsequent erosion and weathering have exposed the central igneous volcanic cores (known locally as sucs), and these dot the landscape through which the first part of the Loire flows – Gerbier de Jonc being a particularly well-formed example. This collision of plates also caused rippling of the landmass to the north, creating a series of calcareous ridges. After leaving the Massif Central, the Loire flows down between these ridges, forming a wide basin with outcrops of chalk and limestone. Where the river has cut down through the ridges, tufa limestone cliffs abut the river and these have been extensively quarried for building stone.

The Loire is a *fleuve sauvage* (untamed river), the level of water fluctuating greatly between seasons. In summer large sandbanks appear, while in winter riverside meadows are flooded. The river is fed by a number of important tributaries including the Allier, Cher, Indre and Vienne (all of which rise in the Massif Central) and the Loir, Sarthe and Maine which drain the hills of Normandy.

Wildlife

While a number of small mammals (including rabbits, hares, red squirrels, voles, water rats and weasels) may be

Roe deer crossing the track near Avaray (Stage 17)

seen scuttling across the track, this is not an area inhabited by wild animals – with two exceptions. Large forests close to the river were once reserved for royal hunting parties seeking bears, wolves, wild boar and deer. Bears and wolves were wiped out long ago, but deer and boar are still present.

There is a wide range of birdlife. White swans, geese and many varieties of ducks inhabit the river and its banks. Cruising above, raptors, particularly buzzards and kites, are frequently seen hunting small mammals. Birds that live by fishing include cormorants, noticeable when perched on rocks with their wings spread out to dry, and grey herons, which can be seen standing in shallow water waiting to strike or stalking purposefully along the banks. Egrets are commonly seen in fields where they often pick fleas off cattle. Seasonal sandbanks and islands in the Loire attract millions of migratory birds during summer months and some have become protected reserves.

PREPARATION

When to go
With the exception of Stage 1 in the Massif Central, where snow can remain on the ground until late April, the route is generally cyclable from April to October. If the source is inaccessible, an alternative would be to start from the beginning of Stage 3 in Le Puy-en-Velay, which can be reached directly by train.

How long will it take?
The route has been broken into 26 stages, averaging 41km per stage. A fit cyclist, cycling an average of 80km/day should be able to complete the route in under a fortnight. If travelling at a gentler pace of 50km/day and allowing time for sightseeing, cycling the Loire to the Atlantic coast would take three weeks. There are many places to stay along the route, making it easy to tailor daily distances to your requirements.

What kind of cycle is suitable?
Most of the route is on asphalt cycle tracks or alongside quiet country roads. However, there are some stretches with gravel surfaces and although these are invariably well graded, posing no problems for most kinds of cycle, cycling the Loire is not recommended for narrow-tyred racing cycles. The most suitable type of cycle is either a touring cycle or a hybrid (a lightweight but strong cross between a touring cycle and a mountain bike, with at least 21 gears). There is no advantage in using a mountain bike. Front suspension is beneficial as it absorbs much of the vibration. Straight handlebars, with bar-ends enabling you to vary your position regularly, are recommended. Make sure your cycle is serviced and lubricated before you

Fully equipped cycle and free air for cyclists at Savonnières (Stage 20)

start – particularly the brakes, gears and chain.

As important as the cycle is your choice of tyres. Slick road tyres are not suitable and knobbly mountain bike tyres not necessary. What you need is something in-between with good tread and a slightly wider profile than you would use for everyday cycling at home. To reduce the chance of punctures, choose tyres with puncture-resistant armouring, such as a Kevlar™ band.

GETTING THERE AND BACK

By rail
The start of the route on the slopes of Gerbier de Jonc is not directly accessible by public transport. There are railway stations east of the start at Livron

in the Rhone Valley (82km away with 1331m ascent) and west of the start at Langogne (51km with 825m ascent). Both these options require long rides with substantial amounts of ascent. The average cyclist should set aside a day to reach Gerbier de Jonc. There is a bus service that carries cycles (route E12) from Valence bus station in the Rhone Valley that runs up to Le Cheylard, more than halfway along the route from Livron. From Le Cheylard it is 31km to the start with 989m ascent. Buses operate five times daily on weekdays (three Sat, two Sun) from 1 April to 30 November, with a journey time of 90 minutes. For booking tel +33 09 70 82 15 60 – 48hr notice required. Details can be found at www.auvergnerhonealpes.fr/interurbainardeche.

The routes to the source from Le Cheylard and Langogne are described in detail in the Prologue.

Valence Ville station is on the old Rhone Valley main line between Lyon and Marseille and is served by trains every hour from Lyon Part Dieu or every two hours from Marseille St Charles. Note that Valence TGV station is 10km NE of Valence, with a connecting service linking it to Valence Ville. Langogne is served by trains between Clermont-Ferrand and Nîmes, but there are only three services per day on this line.

Travelling from the UK, you can take your cycle on Eurostar from London St Pancras (not Ebbsfleet nor Ashford) to Paris (Gare du Nord). Trains run hourly throughout the day, taking less than two and a half hours to reach Paris via the Channel tunnel. Up to six cycles are carried per train: two fully assembled, plus four dismantled bikes packed in specially designed fibre-glass bike boxes provided by Eurostar. Bookings, which open six months in advance, must be made through EuroDespatch (+44 (0)344 822 5822). Prices vary from £30 to £55 depending on how far ahead you book and whether your cycle is fully assembled or dismantled. Cycles must be checked in at the EuroDespatch centre beside the bus drop-off point at the back of St Pancras station, at least 60min before departure. If you need to dismantle your bike, EuroDespatch will provide tools and packing advice. Leave yourself plenty of time for dismantling and packing. In Paris Gare du Nord, cycles are collected from Geoparts baggage office which is reached by a path L of platform 3. More information at www.eurostar.com. Unfortunately the direct

Loading cycles on the Interloire train at St Nazaire (Stage 26)

CROSSING PARIS

After arrival in Paris you need to cycle from Gare du Nord to Gare de Lyon (4km) or Gare de Bercy (5.5km) following a series of wide avenues. Go ahead opposite main entrance to Gare du Nord along semi-pedestrianised Bvd de Denain. At end turn L (Bvd de Magenta) and follow this to reach Pl de la République. Continue round this square and leave on opposite side by Bvd du Temple, becoming Bvd des Filles du Calvaire then Bvd Beaumarchais, to reach Pl de la Bastille. Bear L (passing memorial column to 1830 revolution) then R and fork R on cycle track beside Bvd de la Bastille with canal St Martin R. Turn L beside building 16, following Rue de Bercy past **Gare de Lyon** station L and under modernistic Ministry of Finance building. Pass Accor indoor arena R then turn L (Rue Corbineau) and take lift on R up to **Gare de Bercy**.

Eurostar service to Lyon, Valence and Marseille does not carry cycles.

There are frequent TGV high-speed trains from Paris to Lyon, but few have cycle spaces. The SNCF (French railways) website www.sncf-connect.com can be used to identify which trains carry bikes and to make reservations. If no TGV is available, you can take a TER regional train from Paris Bercy to Lyon. Bicycles are carried free on these trains with no reservations required

Provision of cycle space on European trains changes frequently. Up-to-date information on travelling by train with a cycle can be found at a website dedicated to worldwide rail travel, 'The man in seat 61' (www.seat61.com).

By air
Airports at Lyon (which requires an 18km cycle to Lyon Part Dieu station for an hourly train to Valence Ville) and Marseille (hourly trains taking two hours to Valence Ville, or three trains daily taking 4–5 hours to Langogne via Nîmes), can be used to access the Loire source. Airlines have different requirements regarding how cycles are presented and some, but not all, make a charge, which you should pay when booking as it is usually greater at the airport. All require tyres partially deflated, handlebars turned and pedals removed (loosen pedals beforehand to make them easier to remove at the airport). Most will accept your cycle in a transparent polythene bike-bag, although some insist on use of a cardboard bike-box. Excess Baggage Company counters at Heathrow and Gatwick sell cardboard bike boxes (www.left-baggage.co.uk). Away from the airports, boxes can be obtained from cycle shops, sometimes for free. You do, however, then have the problem of how to get the box to the airport.

By road

If you're lucky enough to have some-one prepared to drive you to the start, Gerbier de Jonc is on the D378 close to its junction with the D116 and D237 in the Ardèche département of France (44°50′29″N, 04°13′08″E; 31T 596317E, 4966063N). With your own vehicle the most convenient place to leave it is Tours, from where trains can be used to reach Valence or Langogne on the outward journey, and which can be reached by train from St Nazaire on the return. Tours is about 525km from Calais.

European Bike Express operates a coach service with dedicated cycle trailer from Northern England, pick-ing up en route across England to the Mediterranean, with a drop-off point at Valence. Details and booking through www.bike-express.co.uk.

Intermediate access

There are international airports at St Étienne (Stage 5), Tours (Stage 18) and Nantes (Stage 24). After St Étienne much of the route is closely followed by railway lines; stations en route are listed in the text. From mid June to mid September SNCF run Interloire cycle trains daily between Orléans and Le Croisic (west of St Nazaire). These have enhanced capacity for cycles at no extra charge, and call at Blois, St Pierre-des-Corps (for Tours), Saumur, Angers, Ancenis, Nantes and St Nazaire. Find details at www.loire-a-velo.fr.

Getting home

The nearest station to St Brevin-les-Pins is St Nazaire, 9km away on the opposite side of the Loire estuary. Details on how to reach the station are given at the end of Stage 26. TGV Atlantique services, some of which carry cycles, run from St Nazaire to Paris Montparnasse station, some-times requiring a change in Nantes. It is then necessary to cycle through the middle of Paris to reach Gare du Nord and catch a Eurostar train to London. Cycle check-in at Gare du Nord is at the Geoparts office (follow the path to the left of platform 3) at least one hour before departure.

Alternatively, you can travel by regional trains that carry cycles to St Malo (via Nantes and Rennes), from where daily ferry services sail to Portsmouth (Brittany Ferries: www.brittany-ferries.co.uk) or Poole via the Channel Islands (Condor Ferries: www.condorferries.co.uk).

NAVIGATION

Maps

There is no specific cycling map that covers the whole route. From the source to Digoin (Stages 1–7) it is nec-essary to rely on the maps in this book or use general road and leisure maps. The most suitable road maps are:

Michelin (1:150,000)
• 331 Ardèche, Haute-Loire
• 327 Loire, Rhône

Waymarks followed (clockwise from top left): Vivez la Loire Sauvage, Véloire V71, EuroVelo EV6, Loire à Vélo, provisional or temporary route sign.

IGN (1:100,000)
- 156 Le Puy-en-Velay, Privas
- 149 Lyon, St Étienne
- 141 Moulins, Vichy

Below Digoin (Stage 8 onwards) the route is mapped by the first four sheets of the definitive series of 1:100,000 strip maps of EuroVelo EV6, published by Huber Kartographie. These can be purchased separately or as a set of six

which includes two additional maps showing the route of EV6 through eastern France to Basle.

Huber Kartographie, La Loire à Vélo (1:100,000)
- sheet 4 Belleville-sur-Loire– Paray-le-Monial
- sheet 3 Blois–Belleville-sur-Loire
- sheet 2 Angers–Blois
- sheet 1 Atlantique–Angers

Various online maps are available to download, at a scale of your choice. Particularly useful is Open Street Map, www.openstreetmap.org, which has a cycle route option showing the routes of both La Loire à Vélo and EV6. There are specific websites dedicated to Loire à Vélo and EV6 which include definitive route maps and details about accommodation and refreshments, points of interest, tourist offices and cycle shops. These can be found at www.loireavelo.fr and www.eurovelo.com/ev6/france.

Waymarking
The first four stages from Gerbier de Jonc to Aurec approximately follow a regional cycle route waymarked as 'Vivez la Loire Sauvage'. Between Le Brignon (mid-Stage 2) and Lavoûte-sur-Loire (mid-Stage 3) the route follows the planned itinerary of French national véloroute V73 and waymarking will eventually reflect this. From Lavoûte to St Yan (most of Stages 3–7), the 'Véloire' V71 véloroute is followed. This is in development and is unwaymarked until Montrond-les-Bains (mid-Stage 5), from where V71 waymarks take you on to St Yan near Digoin. After Digoin, EuroVelo route EV6 is followed, and at Cuffy near Nevers (Stage 11) this is joined by a French national route waymarked as 'La Loire à Vélo' (LV). Although these two routes then run together to St Brevin-les-Pins opposite St Nazaire, waymarking is predominantly Loire à Vélo. Route development and

waymarking vary between départements. In the introduction to each stage an indication is given of the predominant waymarks followed.

The first part of the route before Nevers often follows local roads. These are numbered as département roads (D roads). However, the numbering system can be confusing. Responsibility for roads in France has been devolved from national to local government, with responsibility for many former *routes nationales* (N roads) being transferred to local départements. This has resulted in most being renumbered as D roads. As départements have different systems of numbering, D road numbers often change when crossing département boundaries.

Summary of cycle routes followed		
	Vivez la Loire Sauvage	Stages 1–4
V73		Stage 2
V71	Véloire	Stages 5–7
EV6	EuroVelo 6	Stages 8–10
LV	Loire à Vélo	Stages 11–26

Guidebooks
There are four published guidebooks, but these only cover Stages 11–26 between Nevers and St Nazaire and none are in English. In French, Chamina Edition publish *La Loire à Vélo* with strip maps at 1:100,000, Editions Ouest-France publish *L'Intégrale de la Loire à Vélo* by Michel

Bonduelle and Le Routard publish *La Loire à Vélo*. In German, Esterbauer Bikeline publish *Loire-Radweg*, a *radtourenbuch und karte* cycle tour guidebook with maps at 1:75,000.

There are a number of general touring guides to the Loire, including those from Michelin Green Guides (*Château of the Loire*) and Dorling Kindersley Eyewitness Travel (*Loire Valley*).

Most of these maps and guidebooks are available from leading bookshops including Stanfords, London and The Map Shop, Upton upon Severn. Relevant maps are widely available en route.

Many hotels and guest houses display 'Cyclists Welcome' signs

ACCOMMODATION

Hotels, guest houses and bed & breakfast

For most of the route there is a wide variety of accommodation. The stage descriptions identify places known to have accommodation, but they are not exhaustive. Hotels vary from expensive five-star properties to modest local establishments and usually offer a full meal service. Guest houses and bed & breakfast accommodation, known as *chambres d'hôte* in French, generally offer only breakfast. Tourist information offices will often telephone for you and make local reservations. After hours, some tourist offices display a sign outside showing local establishments with vacancies. Booking ahead is seldom

necessary, except on popular stages in high season, although it is advisable to start looking for accommodation soon after 1600. Most properties are cycle-friendly and will find you a secure overnight place for your pride and joy. *Accueil Vélo* (cyclists welcome) is a national quality mark displayed by establishments within 5km of the route that welcome cyclists and provide facilities including overnight cycle storage.

Prices for accommodation in France are similar to, or slightly cheaper than, prices in the UK.

Youth hostels and gîtes d'étape

France has two youth hostel associations, the FUAJ and the LFAJ, who operate four official youth hostels on or near the route. These are listed

Most accommodation has secure storage for cycles, like this cycle garage in Gien (Stage 14)

in Appendix C. In addition there are independent backpackers' hostels in some of the larger towns and cities. To use an official youth hostel you need to be a member of an association affiliated to Hostelling International (YHA in England, SYHA in Scotland). Unlike British hostels, most European hostels do not have self-catering facilities but do provide good value hot meals. Hostels get very busy, particularly during school holidays, and booking is advised through www.hihostels.com. Details of independent hostels can be found at www.hostelbookers.com.

Gîtes d'étape are hostels and rural refuges in France for walkers and cyclists. They are mostly found in mountain areas, although there are an increasing number along the Loire Valley. A listing of French gîtes d'étape can be found at www.gites-refuges.com. Do not confuse these with *Gîtes de France*, which are rural properties rented as weekly holiday homes.

Camping

If you are prepared to carry all the necessary equipment, camping is the cheapest way of cycling the Loire. The stage descriptions identify many official campsites but these are not exhaustive. Camping may be possible in other locations with the permission of local landowners.

FOOD AND DRINK

Where to eat

There are thousands of places where cyclists can eat and drink, varying from snack bars, *crêperies* and local inns to Michelin-starred restaurants. Locations of many places to eat are listed in stage descriptions, but these are by no means exhaustive. Days and times of opening vary. When planning your day, try to be flexible, as some inns and small restaurants do not open at lunchtime. An *auberge* is a local inn offering food and drink. English-language menus may be available in big cities and tourist areas, but are less common in smaller towns and rural locations.

When to eat

Breakfast (*petit déjeuner*) is usually continental: breads, jam and a hot drink. Traditionally lunch (*déjeuner*) was the main meal of the day, although this is slowly changing, and is unlikely to prove suitable if you plan an afternoon in the saddle. Most restaurants offer a *menu du jour* at lunchtime: a three-course set meal that usually offers very good value for money. It is often hard to find light meals/snacks in bars or restaurants, and if you want a light lunch you may need to purchase items such as sandwiches, quiche Lorraine or *croque-monsieur* (a toasted ham and cheese sandwich) from a bakery.

For dinner (*dîner*) a wide variety of cuisine is available. Much of what is available is pan-European and will be easily recognisable. There are, however, national and regional dishes you may wish to try. Historically, French restaurants offered only fixed-price set menus with two, three or more courses. This is slowly changing and most restaurants nowadays offer both fixed-price and à la carte menus.

What to eat

France is widely regarded as a place where the preparation and presentation of food is central to the country's culture. Modern-day French cuisine was first codified by Georges Escoffier in *Le Guide Culinaire* (1903). Central to Escoffier's method was the use of light sauces made from stocks and broths to enhance the flavour of the

Creamy coloured Charolais cattle graze the Charolais hills (Stage 9)

dish, in place of heavy sauces that had previously been used to mask the taste of bad meat. French cooking was further refined in the 1960s with the arrival of *nouvelle cuisine*, which sought to simplify techniques, lessen cooking time and preserve natural flavours by changing cooking methods.

By contrast, traditional cooking of the Auvergne is rustic fare, mostly combining cheaper cuts of pork with potatoes and basic vegetables, including *soupe aux chou* (cabbage, pork and potato soup), *potée Auvergnate* (hotpot of pork, potatoes and vegetables) and *truffade* (cheese, garlic and potato pancake). The crisp mountain air of the higher parts of the Auvergne is perfect for drying hams and sausages. One particular speciality is *lentilles vertes*, green lentils from Le Puy-en-Velay used in soup or served with duck, goose or sausage dishes. Local cheeses include *bleu d'Auvergne*, Cantal and St Nectaire, while *tarte aux myrtilles* is a traditional dessert made with bilberries from the mountains.

Burgundy in central France is famous not only for its eponymous red wine but also for beef from Charolais cattle, poultry from Bourg-en-Bresse, mustard from Dijon and cheese made with the milk from Salers cattle. This is reflected in regional cuisine, particularly *bœuf Bourguignon* (beef slow-cooked in red wine) and *coq au vin* (chicken casseroled in red wine). Other specialities include *escargots à la Bourgogne* (snails in garlic and

parsley butter) and *lapin à la moutarde* (rabbit in mustard sauce).

The food of Pays de la Loire is more elegant, reflecting perhaps the regal history of the region. Freshwater fish (including pike, carp and salmon), often served with *beurre blanc* (white wine and butter sauce), are plentiful inland, while sea fish and shellfish, particularly *huîtres* (oysters), abound near the Atlantic. *Carrelet* (flounder) are caught in the Loire estuary. Châteaubriand steak (a thick cut from the tenderloin fillet) is named after a small village. Other meat dishes include *rillauds d'Anjou* (fried pork belly) and muscatel sausages. Caves in riverside cliffs are widely used to cultivate mushrooms, which appear in many dishes. Desserts include *gâteau Pithiviers* (puff pastry and almond paste tart). A long history of sugar refining and biscuit making has given Nantes such specialities as *berlingot Nantais* (multicoloured pyramid-shaped sugar sweets), shortbreads and *Petit Beurre* biscuits.

What to drink
The lower and middle Loire Valley hosts a string of wine-producing districts, many producing good vin de pays wines, but there are some well-known appellations. Most wine is white but there are some areas producing non-appellation soft red wines from gamay or pinot noir grapes. There is a wide contrast in styles, with dry (often very dry) whites being produced in the east and west

The green-verbena flavoured Verveine du Velay is made in Le Puy-en-Velay (Stage 2)

while sweeter whites, rosés and softer reds are produced in the central part between Orléans and Angers.

The first appellations encountered are Pouilly and Sancerre, two villages that face each other across the middle Loire (Stage 12). Here, sauvignon blanc grapes are used to produce flinty dry white wines, recommended to be drunk with shellfish. Further downriver, between Amboise and Tours, are the Touraine appellation districts of Vouvray and Montlouis (Stage 19) where chenin blanc grapes produce dry, sweet and sparkling white wines. In the districts of Chinon and Bourgueil (Stage 21), cabernet franc grapes are used to make soft Beaujolais-style red wine, usually served chilled. Slightly downriver, Saumur (Stage 21) is a light and fruity red. Anjou wine comes from an area just south of Angers (Stage 23). Here again chenin blanc grapes produce mostly sweet white wine, although the district is best known for rosé wine and vin gris (white wine made from red grapes) using cabernet franc grapes. The largest of the Loire's wine-producing appellations is that of Muscadet between Ancenis and Nantes (Stages 24–26). Muscadet is the name of a grape, unique to this area, which produces a very dry white wine with low acidity, perfect for serving with fish or seafood.

Particular apéritifs and digestifs from the Loire include yellow *gentiane* from Auvergne and green *verveine du Velay* made near Le Puy from verbena. The blackcurrant liqueur Crème de Cassis comes from

35

Burgundy, while orange-flavoured Cointreau is distilled near Angers (Stage 22). Chambord is a blackberry and raspberry liqueur produced in the Loire Valley since 1982, based on a favourite drink of Louis XIV.

Although central France is predominantly a wine-drinking region, beer (*bière*) is widely consumed. Draught beer (*une pression*) is usually available in two main styles: *blonde* (European-style lager) or *blanche* (partly cloudy wheat beer). Beer is normally sold in 250mm glasses; for a larger 500mm glass you should ask for a *cinquante* which is often called a 'pint'.

All the usual soft drinks (colas, lemonade, fruit juices, mineral waters) are widely available. In the Auvergne, mineral water naturally filtered through the volcanic rocks of the Massif Central is a major industry with well-known brands including Badoit, Volvic and Vichy.

AMENITIES AND SERVICES

Grocery shops

All cities, towns and larger villages cycled through have grocery stores and often supermarkets, and most have pharmacies. Almost every village has a *boulangerie* (bakery) that is open from early morning and bakes fresh bread several times a day. Shop opening hours vary and in southern France many shops close in the afternoon between 1300 and 1600.

Cycle shops

The route is well provided with cycle shops, most with repair facilities. Locations are listed in the stage descriptions, although this is not exhaustive. Many cycle shops will adjust brakes and gears, or lubricate your chain, while you wait, often not seeking reimbursement for minor repairs. Touring cyclists should not abuse this generosity and always offer to pay, even if this is refused.

Banks and currency exchange

France switched from French francs to €uros in 2002. Almost every town has a bank and most have ATM machines which enable you to make transactions in English. However, very few offer over-the-counter currency exchange. In major cities like Orléans, Tours and Nantes, there are commercial exchange bureaux, but in other locations the only way to obtain currency is to use ATM machines to withdraw cash from your personal account. Contact your bank to activate your bank card for use in Europe, or put cash on a travel card for use abroad.

Telephone and internet

The whole route has mobile phone coverage. Contact your network provider to ensure your phone is enabled for foreign use with the optimum price package. The international dialling code from the UK (+44) to France is +33.

Almost all hotels, guest houses and hostels and many restaurants make internet access available to guests, usually free of charge.

Electricity
Voltage is 220v, 50HzAC. Plugs are standard European two-pin round.

WHAT TO TAKE

Clothing and personal items
Even though the route is predominantly downhill, weight should be kept to a minimum. You will need clothes for cycling (shoes, socks, shorts/trousers, shirt, fleece, waterproofs) and clothes for evenings and days off. The best maxim is two of each: 'one to wear, one to wash'. Time of year makes a difference as you need more and warmer clothing in April/May and September/October. All of this clothing should be washable en route, and a small tube or bottle of travel wash is useful. A sun hat and sunglasses are essential, while gloves and a woolly hat are advisable except in high summer.

In addition to your usual toiletries you will need sun cream and lip salve. You should take a simple first-aid kit. If staying in hostels you will need a towel and torch (your cycle light should suffice for the latter).

Cycle equipment
Everything you take needs to be carried on your cycle. If overnighting in accommodation, a pair of rear panniers should be sufficient to carry all your clothing and equipment, although if camping, you may also need front panniers. Panniers should be 100% watertight. If in doubt, pack everything inside a strong polythene lining bag. Rubble bags, obtainable from builders' merchants, are ideal for this purpose. A bar-bag is a useful way of carrying items you need to access quickly such as maps, sunglasses, camera, spare tubes, puncture kit and tools. A transparent map case attached to the top of your bar-bag is an ideal way of displaying maps and guidebook.

Your cycle should be fitted with mudguards and bell, and be capable of carrying water bottles, pump and lights. Many cyclists fit an odometer to measure distances. A basic tool kit should consist of puncture repair kit, spanners, Allen keys, adjustable spanner, screwdriver, spoke key and chain repair tool. The only essential spares are two spare tubes. On a long cycle ride, sometimes on dusty tracks, your chain will need regular lubrication; you should either carry a can of spray-lube or make regular visits to cycle shops. A good strong lock is advisable.

SAFETY AND EMERGENCIES

Weather
Stage 1 is exposed to mountain weather, with winter snowfall that can remain on the ground until April. The rest of the route is in the cool temperate zone with warm summers, cool winters and year-round moderate

Average temperatures (max/min °C)							
	Apr	May	Jun	Jul	Aug	Sep	Oct
Le Puy	6/0	11/5	15/8	18/10	18/11	13/7	9/4
Orléans	16/5	20/9	23/11	26/13	26/14	22/10	17/8
Nantes	16/6	20/10	23/12	25/14	26/13	22/11	18/9

Average rainfall (mm/rainy days)							
	Apr	May	Jun	Jul	Aug	Sep	Oct
Le Puy	125/16	127/15	72/12	42/10	52/13	153/13	232/19
Orléans	42/17	50/16	38/14	55/14	47/12	46/14	58/20
Nantes	60/20	57/18	39/15	43/17	42/16	51/17	91/23

rainfall which increases for the last few stages as you near the Atlantic.

Road safety
Throughout the route, cycling is on the right side of the road. If you have never cycled before on the right you will quickly adapt, but roundabouts may prove challenging. You are most prone to mistakes when setting off each morning. France is a very cycle-friendly country; drivers will normally give you plenty of space when overtaking and often wait

Contra-flow cycling is often permitted on one-way streets

behind patiently until space to pass is available.

Much of the route is on dedicated cycle paths, although care is necessary as these are sometimes shared with pedestrians. Use your bell, politely, when approaching pedestrians from behind. Where you are required to cycle on the road there is often a dedicated cycle lane.

Many city and town centres have pedestrian-only zones. These restrictions are often only loosely enforced and you may find locals cycling within them – indeed, many zones have signs allowing cycling. One-way streets often have signs permitting contra-flow cycling.

France does not require compulsory wearing of cycle helmets, although their use is recommended. Improved ventilation has made wearing modern lightweight helmets more comfortable.

Emergencies

In the unlikely event of an accident, the standardised EU emergency phone number is 112. The entire route has mobile phone coverage. Provided you have a European Health Insurance Card (EHIC) issued by an EU country or a GHIC card issued to UK citizens, medical costs are covered under reciprocal health insurance agreements – although you may have to pay for an ambulance and claim the cost back through insurance.

Theft

In general the route is safe and the risk of theft very low. However, you should always lock your cycle and watch your belongings, especially in cities.

Insurance

Travel insurance policies usually cover you when cycle touring, but they do not normally cover damage to, or theft of, your bicycle. If you have a household contents policy, this may cover cycle theft, but limits may be less than the real cost of your cycle. Cycling UK (formerly the Cyclists' Touring Club) has a policy tailored to the needs of cycle tourists (www.cyclinguk.org).

ABOUT THIS GUIDE

Text and maps

There are 26 stages, each covered by maps drawn to a scale of 1:150,000. These maps have been produced specially for this guide and, when combined with the detailed stage descriptions, it is possible to follow the route without the expense or weight of carrying a large number of other maps, particularly after Nevers where signposting and waymarking is excellent. Beware, however, as the route described here does not always follow the waymarked route exactly. GPX files are freely available to anyone who has bought this guide on Cicerone's website at www.cicerone. co.uk/1083/gpx.

Gradient profiles are provided for Stages 1–6, the hillier part of the route. After Roanne there are few hills and, except for an alternative route that goes uphill to Sancerre (Stage 12), no ascents of over 50m are encountered.

Place names on the maps that are significant for route navigation are shown in **bold** in the text. The abbreviation 'sp' in the text indicates a signpost. Distances shown are cumulative within each stage. For each city/town/village passed, an indication is given of facilities available (accommodation, refreshments, YH, camping, tourist office, cycle shop, station) when the guide was written. This information is neither exhaustive nor does it guarantee that establishments are still in business. No attempt has been made to list all such facilities, as this would require another book of the same size. For full listing of accommodation, contact local tourist offices. Such listings are usually available online. Tourist offices along the route are listed in Appendix B.

Although route descriptions were accurate at the time of writing, things do change. Temporary diversions may be necessary to circumnavigate improvement works and permanent diversions may be necessary

to incorporate new sections of cycle track. Some sections are waymarked as *provisoire* (provisional) where work to provide a separate cycle route is ongoing. If construction is in progress you may find signs showing recommended diversions, although these are likely to be in French only. Deviations, temporary and provisional routes are waymarked with yellow signs.

Some alternative routes exist. Where these offer a reasonable variant, usually because they visit somewhere popular just off-route or have less traffic or offer a better surface, they are mentioned in the text and shown in blue on the maps.

Language

French is spoken throughout the route, although many people – especially in the tourism industry – speak at least a few words of English. In this guide, French names are used with the exception of Bourgogne and Bretagne, where the English Burgundy and Brittany are preferred. The French word château covers a wide variety of buildings, from royal palaces and stately homes to local manor houses and medieval castles. See Appendix E for a glossary of French terms that may be useful along the route.

THE LOIRE
CYCLE ROUTE

Ruined castle at Trèves, said to be Sir Lancelot's birthplace (Stage 22)

PROLOGUE

Getting to the start

Start	Le Cheylard (442m) or Langogne (914m)
Finish	Gerbier de Jonc, Geographic Loire source (1409m)
Distance	31.5km from Le Cheylard, 50.5km from Langogne
Waymarking	None

If you arrive by bus at Le Cheylard, or train at Langogne, the following directions will take you to the start of the route proper at the Geographic Loire source. Both routes include steep ascents.

From Le Cheylard

From terminus of route E12 bus from Valence at Ave Saunier in **Le Cheylard** (442m) (accommodation, refreshments, camping, tourist office), follow D120 NE (Ave de Saunier, sp La Voulte sur Rhône) downhill for 150m. ◄ Turn L (D578, sp Lamastre) across bridge over river Eyrieux. Bear R into Ave de la Gare, and just before pedestrian crossing turn sharply R (Ch d'Aurives) downhill on narrow lane towards riverbank. Turn R under bridge (Voie des Boutières) and fork R to continue out of village.

Ignore the signpost pointing L to Gerbier de Jonc.

You are now on well-surfaced cycle track along route of old railway line cut into valley side. This track is followed for 7km past Riotord and derelict bridge (both L) to reach beginning of St Martin-de-Valamas. Emerge onto asphalt road and follow this bearing R, and turn immediately L at T-junction. Bear L on tree-lined road to cross river bridge then turn R (D120) uphill into **St Martin-de-Valamas** (8km, 551m) (accommodation, refreshments, camping, tourist office).

Where road turns sharply R at hairpin bend, turn L (D237, sp Gerbier de Jonc) and follow D237 for 22.5km,

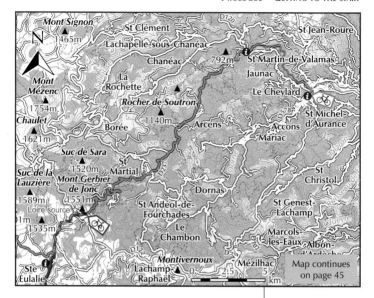

at first climbing gently through Valamas (10km, 564m) and **Arcens** (14.5km, 626m) (accommodation, refreshments, camping) along the Eysse valley.

After Arcens, road climbs steadily through forest, passing junction with D337 road R (18.5km, 700m), after which climb becomes steeper. Ascend through La Chazotte hamlet to reach **St Martial** (21.5km, 885m) (refreshments, camping), which sits on hillside overlooking pretty lake. Turn sharply L in village (sp Gerbier de Jonc) and climb steeply through forest round a series of seven hairpin bends.

Pass La Chaumette L (accommodation) then emerge above forest to reach T-junction on top of ridge with rugged cone of Gerbier de Jonc rising R and views in all directions (31km, 1417m). ▶ Turn R (D378, sp Les Estables), passing linear car park, to reach cluster of buildings at La Source Géographique de la Loire L, opposite footpath to summit of **Mont Gerbier de Jonc**, R (accommodation, refreshments).

At the top of the ridge, the route crosses the ligne de partage des eaux (watershed) between the Mediterranean and Atlantic drainage basins, indicated by a sign on the L.

43

From Langogne

Turn L outside **Langogne** station (914m) (accommodation, refreshments, camping, tourist office, station) into Ave de la Gare, and L again under railway bridge (N88, sp Le Puy). Follow this over river Allier and continue for 8km, winding through **Pradelles** (7km, 1159m) (accommodation, refreshments, camping) to reach major road junction. Turn sharply R (N102, sp Aubenas) and after 3km turn L (D110, sp Coucouron) (11km, 1293m).

Descend gently across plateau to **Coucouron** (19km, 1165m) (accommodation, refreshments, camping) and

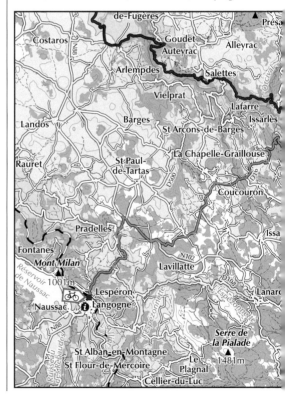

turn sharply R at roundabout (D16, sp Le Béage). Follow road through **La Chapelle-Graillouse** (23.5km, 1112m) and wind downhill through forest to cross Pont de la Borie bridge over Loire (28.5km, 893m). Climb up other side of valley and pass roundabout with turn-off for Lac-d'Issarlès on R (accommodation, refreshments, camping, tourist office). ▶

Continue ahead, ascending to reach **Le Béage** (38.5km, 1220m) (accommodation, refreshments). Turn R (D122, sp Gerbier de Jonc) and after 250m turn R again. Continue across high plateau to reach road

The route from the source returns via Lac-d'Issarlès. If you're planning to stay the night here you could drop your bags off and cycle up to the source and back unencumbered.

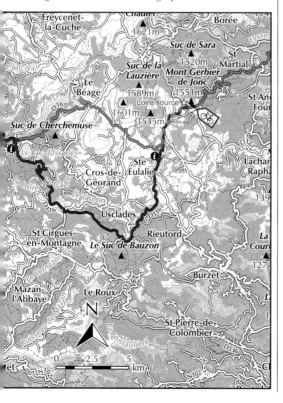

La Source Géographique de la Loire is in a cowshed below Mt Gerbier de Jonc

junction (47km, 1240m). Turn L (D116), ascending with small Loire stream on R and turn L on side road to reach cluster of buildings at La Source Géographique de la Loire (50.5km, 1409m) (accommodation, refreshments), beneath summit of **Mont Gerbier de Jonc**.

The Loire rises at **three little springs** dotted along the southern slopes of Mont Gerbier de Jonc (1551m), a rocky outcrop formed from the plug of a long-extinct volcano that rises above the surrounding countryside. These three sources go by the names (from west to east) of La Source Authentique (genuine source), La Source Géographique (geographic source) and La Source Véritable (true source). There is little to choose between them and as they line the roadside with only 1km between them all it is possible to visit all three. The road between them is lined with souvenir stalls, craft shops and cafés. The most visited is the middle one (La Source Géographique), which can be found inside a cowshed, and our Loire Cycle Route starts here.

STAGE 1
Gerbier de Jonc to Goudet

Start	Gerbier de Jonc, Geographic Loire source (1409m)
Finish	Goudet bridge (772m)
Distance	50km
Waymarking	Vivez la Loire Sauvage (inconsistent)

The stage starts with a steady descent on quiet country roads through a series of remote villages. After an ascent to the popular crater-lake resort of Lac-d'Issarlès, the route continues through forest above the Loire across a plateau formed by France's last volcanic eruption before descending to the village of Goudet.

From Géographique Loire source at **Mont Gerbier de Jonc**, follow car park exit road SE downhill and turn R (D116), with three little streams that make up the infant Loire cascading down hillside parallel with route. After 2km pass fork L that leads to confluence of source streams and continue downhill with Loire running below L. Bear R (D122) at road junction, then fork L (D116) to reach **Ste Eulalie**

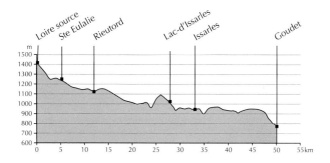

The infant Loire between Ste Eulalie and Rieutord

Zero km stone at the Loire source showing river distance to St Nazaire

(5.5km, 1232m) (accommodation, refreshments, camping, tourist office).

Ste Eulalie (pop 215) is the first village on the Loire and one of the highest villages in the Ardèche. Typical local buildings include the Clastres farm (next to the church), which has a large thatched barn attached to a slate-roofed house and was originally the cloister of a monastery dissolved during the Revolution.

Bear L in village (D116, sp Usclades-et-Rieutord) and descend round hairpin bend to cross Loire and follow river R with cliffs rising L. Re-cross river and pass through hamlet of Sablouze. Turn L at T-junction (D536), crossing Loire again, to reach **Rieutord** (12.5km, 1126m) (refreshments, camping).

Ascend gently away from village and after 1km turn R beside electricity pylon onto quiet side road (sp La Chaplade and déchetterie (rubbish dump)). After 500m, bear L and follow road descending steadily and winding through forest with Loire below R to reach T-junction. Turn R (D160) over river on suspension bridge into hamlet of **La Palisse** (19km, 1018m).

Bear L (D116) to pass through village, then continue alongside Lac Palisse and pass La Palisse **hydro-electric dam** (both L). Continue undulating through forest, with river now below L, then descend steeply round two hairpins to cross bridge over river Gage (949m). Steeply ascend hillside on opposite side of bridge round two more hairpins to reach Col de Gage (1098m) with extensive views. Descend past car parks R to reach beach, hotels and restaurants on shore of **Lac-d'Issarlès** (28km, 1001m) (accommodation, refreshments, camping, tourist office).

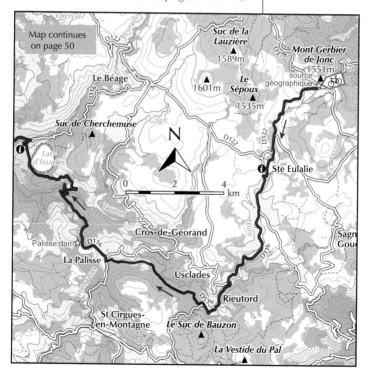

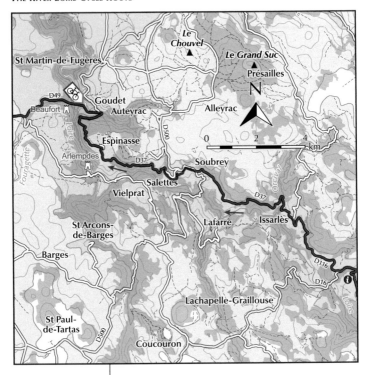

Lac-d'Issarlès (pop 270) is a resort area beside a round crater lake in the mouth of an extinct volcano. With a depth of 138m, making it one of the deepest lakes in France, the high-clarity water appears azure blue. Leisure activities include boating, kayaking, swimming and fishing for brown trout. A circular 3.5km walk goes round the lake.

Continue through older part of village and descend to reach roundabout. Turn L (D16), cross river Veyradeyre and after 1km fork R uphill (D116). Pass through Le Pio hamlet to reach **Issarlès** (34km, 946m) (accommodation, refreshments, camping).

Issarlès (pop 138) sits between the rivers Loire and Orcival on a basalt plateau formed about 10,000 years ago by the last known volcanic activity in France. Traditional granite houses and an 11th-century church are grouped around two shady squares. Dramatic population decline during the 20th century saw the number of residents decline from 2000 (in 1886) to 138 (in 2018).

At end of village, fork L to continue on D116 and descend to cross **river** Orcival, where route enters Haute-Loire département and road number changes to D37. Climb back onto plateau and pass through **Soubrey** hamlet. Cross D500 onto narrow lane that leads to La Viletelle. ▶ Continue through hamlet, then fork L (ignore road going uphill) continuing on unsurfaced winding lane to **Salettes** (42km, 909m).

Salettes (pop 136) is another village that has seen a dramatic 20th-century population decline, down from 1550 in 1901. Its principal building is St Pierre, the 12th-century Romanesque parish church.

Turn R in village then bear L past *mairie* (town hall) on L and turn immediately R uphill to reach D37 after 400m. Bear L at crossroads then follow road contouring through pine forest and cycle through **Espinasse** (46km, 945m). ▶ Descend steeply through forest round series of hairpins to reach junction with D49 on outskirts of **Goudet**. Continue ahead (D49W) downhill to reach Goudet bridge (50km, 772m) (accommodation, refreshments, camping).

Goudet (pop 58) is an attractive village where many of the properties left empty by population decline have been purchased as second homes. The village square is overlooked by the parish church with an unusual pepper-pot tower surmounted by multi-coloured tiles. The ruins of 13th-century Château Beaufort are perched on a rocky promontory on the

The track between La Viletelle and Salettes is surfaced for a short distance; for an alternative route avoiding the rough track, bear R onto D500 and fork L after 800m onto D37. Re-join the main route 400m beyond Salettes.

Just after Espinasse there is a view, below to the left, of ruined Arlempdes Castle, which is regarded as the first château of many passed by the Loire.

Goudet church has a distinctive pepper-pot tower

opposite side of the Loire. This saw service during both the Hundred Years' War (1337–1453) and the Wars of Religion (1562–1598) but was abandoned after the Revolution. Tourism in Goudet started in 1878 when Robert Louis Stevenson visited the town while writing *Travels with a Donkey in the Cévennes*. Other tourists soon followed in his footsteps and his route is nowadays waymarked as the GR70 Robert Louis Stevenson Trail.

STAGE 2
Goudet to Le Puy-en-Velay

Start	Goudet bridge (772m)
Finish	Le Puy-en-Velay, motorway bridge (632m)
Distance	33km
Waymarking	Vivez la Loire Sauvage (Goudet–Le Brignon), then véloroute V73 (Le Brignon–Le Puy-en-Velay), both inconsistent

A short stage that climbs steeply onto a plateau west of the Loire before following a voie verte descending steadily along the course of an old railway past Solignac and through a series of well-lit tunnels to reach the edge of the pilgrimage city of Le Puy-en-Velay.

From **Goudet** bridge, cross Loire and ascend steeply on road winding through woods past **Château Beaufort** L to reach junction with D54. Bear R (still D49) into hilltop village of **Ussel** (4km, 1027m) (refreshments).

Fork R in village, then turn R opposite cemetery (sp Le Brignon). Continue across basalt plateau and through **Bessarioux**. Follow road ahead to reach **Le Brignon** (10.5km, 953m) (refreshments). At beginning of village turn sharply L (sp Bizac, D541) through fields. Continue

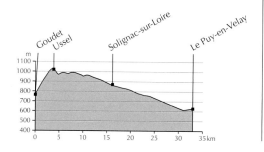

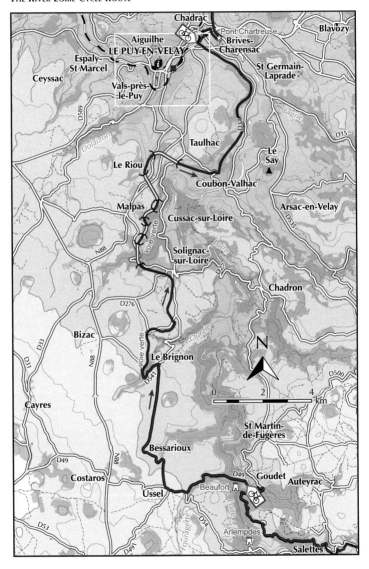

round hairpin bend, crossing Ourzie stream, then after 200m bear R onto voie verte cycle track through woods. This is followed for 5km to pass fire station L and reach crossroads in **Solignac-sur-Loire** (16.5km, 856m) (refreshments).

> **Solignac-sur-Loire** (pop 1275) is a small hilltop town. Little remains of a former castle, most of its site being occupied by the parish church and cemetery. The church was itself badly damaged during the Revolution and rebuilt in the 19th century. Unlike other villages passed, Solignac has a growing population and has become a dormitory settlement for Le Puy-en-Velay.

Continue ahead (Rue de la Ancienne Voie Ferrée, sp Voie Verte) past old station house R, and where road bears R, bear L on gravel track to continue along course of old railway line. Follow voie verte for another 8.5km, descending gently and passing through five tunnels with lighting. Pass hamlet of **Le Riou** (22.5km, 784m) and after last tunnel (**Taulhac**) emerge beside road and bear L behind houses built upon site of former **Coubon-Valhac** station (25.5km, 720m). At complicated crossroads, go ahead past first exit then turn L across main road, circling car park L. Turn R across next road to re-join route of old railway. Continue on voie verte descending gently through woodland then dog-leg L to pass commercial development R on site of former **Brives-Charensac** station (31.5km, 616m) (accommodation, refreshments, camping).

Pass over road bridge, then where railway trackbed ends, go ahead across road and follow zigzag track uphill. ▶ Cross quiet road to reach junction of tracks just before motorway bridge, where stage ends (33km, 632m). To continue onto Stage 3, turn R beside motorway.

To visit Le Puy-en-Velay
Go ahead under motorway bridge and bear L with motorway L and railway R. Continue past roundabout, then fork R (sp Centre Ville) and soon cross road onto cycle

The zigzag track climbs above an old railway cutting that was infilled when a new motorway was built.

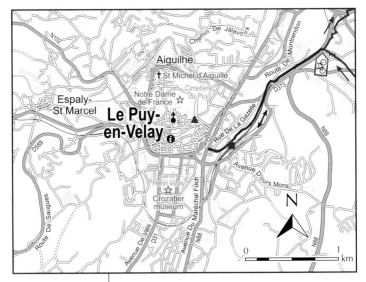

track L. Follow this beside railway L with road below R, then cross road and continue past bus station and railway station (both L). Continue ahead on Ave Charles Dupuy into **Le Puy-en-Velay** (accommodation, refreshments, YH, camping, tourist office, cycle shop, station) (2km off-route).

LE PUY-EN-VELAY

Le Puy-en-Velay (pop 19,000) is both a pilgrimage destination in its own right and a popular start point for the Camino de St Jacques pilgrim route to Santiago in northwest Spain. As a result the town is dominated by religious buildings, with many churches, monasteries, convents and pilgrim hostels. Le Puy sits on top of the basalt core of an extinct volcano, with a number of slender volcanic plugs thrusting skywards, each with a religious edifice on top. The most obvious is the church of St Michel d'Aiguille, balanced precariously on top of a column of rock. From another hilltop the Notre-Dame de France, a gigantic statue of the virgin and child, stares down on the town. Made of iron, it was cast from 213 Russian canons

Notre-Dame de France statue towers over Le Puy-en-Velay cathedral

captured after the siege of Sevastopol (1855). When completed it was the largest statue in the world until surpassed by New York's Statue of Liberty in 1886. Stairs allow visitors to climb inside the statue to a translucent domed viewing gallery in its head. Dominating the old town centre, the zebra-striped cathedral is constructed in alternate bands of creamy sandstone and black basalt. Inside, it houses a black Madonna, a reconstruction of an earlier icon that was destroyed during the Revolution, which is paraded around the town during the feast of Assumption (15 August). Every morning pilgrims gather in the cathedral to be blessed before starting out on their 1500km pilgrimage to Spain.

The traditional industry in Le Puy was lace-making and there are many craft shops and galleries demonstrating lace production and selling lace products. The Crozatier museum has examples of lace items and a gallery of local history. Gastronomically, Le Puy is known for two green products: lentilles vertes are very small dark green, almost black, lentils cultivated on thin volcanic soils. High in protein and low in carbohydrate, they are used in soups and often served to accompany goose, duck and sausage dishes. Green Verveine du Velay is a strong floral liqueur, flavoured with verbena and best consumed ice-cold after a meal.

STAGE 3
Le Puy-en-Velay to Retournac

Start	Le Puy-en-Velay, motorway bridge (632m)
Finish	Retournac, Pl de la République (542m)
Distance	37km
Waymarking	Vivez la Loire Sauvage (inconsistent). Planned véloroutes V73 (Le Puy–Lavoûte) and V71 (Lavoûte–Retournac) are not yet waymarked

This stage mostly follows the 'route des Gorges de la Loire', winding and undulating along the side of a narrow cliff-lined gorge on a quiet main road. A number of tranquil riverside communities are passed before the stage ends at the former lace-making town of Retournac.

The Pont Chartreuse is a much rebuilt 15th-century stone bridge. After floods in 1980 swept part of it away it was restored to its original medieval design.

From just before motorway underbridge between **Brives-Charensac** and **Le Puy-en-Velay**, follow cycle track N beside motorway L (sp Promenades Loire et Borne), descending a series of hairpins. At bottom of hill cross bridge over main road then turn sharply R and R again under motorway. After bridge, turn sharply R on cycle track and follow this, soon passing back under motorway. Continue with Chartreuse monastery (now a school) on hillside R and Loire below L. Turn L onto Pont Chartreuse bridge and cross Loire. ◀

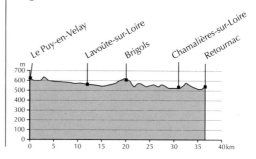

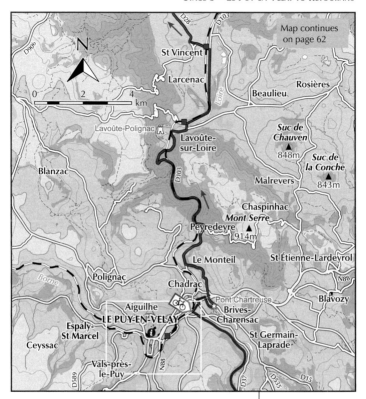

Turn L on main road (D374) and go ahead over round-about (second exit, sp Le Monteil). Pass under motorway then go ahead again at next roundabout (second exit, sp Le Monteil) and follow road ascending past **Le Monteil** (3km, 636m). Descend through short tunnel and turn R at T-junction (D103, sp Lavoûte-sur-Loire) to reach Durianne hamlet. Continue between river L and gorge-side cliffs R and bear L through **Peyredeyre** (6km, 596m).

Pass under railway bridge and continue on road for 7km, winding through narrow gorge between Loire L and railway R, overlooked by rocky cliffs and forested

The route follows a quiet road through a narrow gorge near Peyredeyre

hillsides. After passing under second railway bridge, gorge opens out and **Château de Lavoûte-Polignac** is passed L in bend of Loire. Continue to reach **Lavoûte-sur-Loire** (13km, 562m) (refreshments, camping, station).

> **Lavoûte-sur-Loire** (pop 840) is situated beside a long-established crossing point of the Loire. The current bridge, Pont Neuf, was built in the 19th century, after floods between 1789 and 1870 weakened then destroyed an earlier one. Nearby Château de Lavoûte-Polignac sits on a rocky outcrop overlooking a bend in the Loire. Although a castle has stood here for 1000 years, the current edifice is a result of rebuilding in 1880 after destruction during the Revolution.

Pass church L, then continue on bridge over Loire and bear R out of village, cycling through fields. Pass through **Larcenac** and continue to Le Cros de la Gare (17km, 550m) (station). Turn L opposite building materials depot (Ave de l'Emblaves, sp St Vincent, D251) then cross railway beside **St Vincent** station R and start ascending.

Go ahead at first crossroads (sp Suc de Cèneuil) and turn R at second (Rte du Ramey, D28, sp Suc de Cèneuil) (accommodation). Fork R at triangular junction (sp Cèneuil) then go L ahead at next junction. Fork R, on narrow tree-lined road, steeply uphill into **Brigols** (20.5km, 615m). ▸

This road is a one-way street with contra-flow cycling permitted.

Bear R in village and continue between fields to T-junction. Turn R (D28) then fork immediately L downhill to reach T-junction. Turn L (Ave Philibert Besson, D103) and follow main road bearing R across flower-bedecked bridge over river Arzon into centre of **Vorey-sur-Arzon** (22.5km, 541m) (accommodation, refreshments, camping, tourist office, station).

Continue out of town on D103, ascending past cemetery L, and follow road bearing sharply L then winding through gorge and ascending gently to pass above **Le Chambon** (26.5km, 551m) (refreshments, camping). Beyond village, road passes through short tunnel then crosses bridge high above Loire and continues along gorge side, passing above Chamboulive before descending through **Chamalières-sur-Loire** (31km, 532m) (refreshments, camping, station).

Chamalières-sur-Loire has a 12th-century abbey church that once held a nail from the holy cross

Chamalières-sur-Loire (pop 490) is an attractive riverside village with narrow streets huddled around a Romanesque 12th-century church and the cloisters of a ruined Benedictine abbey, which once claimed to hold a nail from the holy cross. This relic made the abbey a major pilgrimage destination in medieval times. Steady decline during the 16th and 17th centuries, followed by suppression during the Revolution, led to its closure in 1790. Subsequently a small group of nuns inhabited the property until 1943.

After village continue on D103 under railway viaduct and pass station R. Turn R on side road (Ch des Blaches), pass under railway bridge and fork R on narrow lane with views L of ruined hilltop **Château d'Artias**.

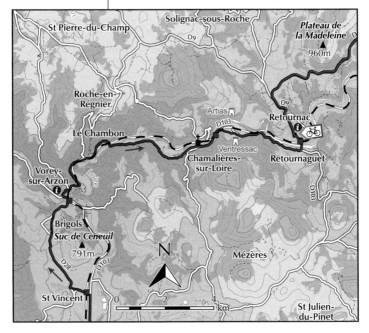

Pass through Ventressac hamlet and bear R onto main road. Road now ascends through forest over small ridge above a meander of the river, before descending into **Retournaguet** (refreshments). Bear L over Loire, pass station L and follow road (D9) winding uphill to reach Pl de la République in centre of **Retournac** (37km, 542m) (accommodation, refreshments, tourist office, station).

Lace-making museum in Retournac teaches lace production skills

> **Retournac** (pop 2950) sits on a hillside 40m above the Loire. A former centre for lace-making, the town houses a museum of lace manufacturing in an old lace mill that has preserved the machinery and patterns of two former producers. In an attempt to keep lace-making skills alive, this collection is used to demonstrate and teach lace production and produce items for sale in the museum shop.

STAGE 4
Retournac to Aurec-sur-Loire

Start	Retournac, Pl de la République (542m)
Finish	Aurec-sur-Loire, pedestrian bridge (429m)
Distance	30km
Waymarking	Vivez la Loire Sauvage (inconsistent). Planned véloroute V71 not yet waymarked

Following country roads, the route climbs 200m above the Loire onto the edge of the basalt plateau and then descends steadily through forest for 9km. After crossing the site of a dried-up lake bed it climbs 100m above the Loire gorge before descending steeply to cross the river by a Himalayan-style suspension bridge into Aurec.

From Pl de la République in **Retournac**, follow Rue de l'Hôtel de Ville (D9) N. Continue onto Rue Baptiste Ribeyron, ascending steadily out of town. After 2km reach road junction and fork R (sp Beauzac, D46). Continue ascending through open country past **Jussac** (3.5km, 672m) and ascend for another 1.5km to reach summit (702m). Descend steadily through forest, passing **La Croix de l'Horme** hamlet where road joins D42, to reach **Beauzac** (11km, 555m) (refreshments, tourist office).

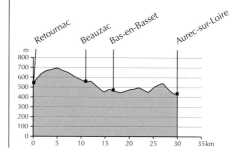

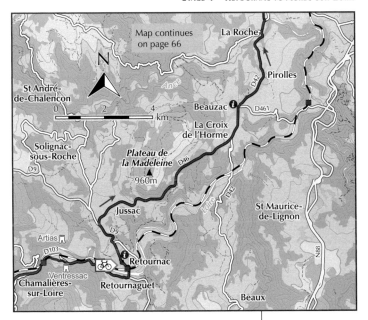

Beauzac (pop 2950) was a rectangular medieval walled town with a castle. Although the castle and walls have mostly been demolished, two medieval gateways have survived and the course of the walls is reflected in the current street layout. The population is growing, with a thriving industrial estate that includes a factory producing St Agur™ processed blue cheese.

Leave town on Rue du Maréchal Leclerc (D42) and continue past industrial area into open country. Pass **Pirolles** R and descend to cross bridge over river Ance into **La Roche** (refreshments).

Fork L at roundabout (second exit, sp Aurec, D425). After 350m, fork L (Rte de Beauzac), continuing downhill. Pass St Vincent de Paul chapel L and continue ahead on narrow road (Rue St Vincent de Paul). Bear R into Pl de la Marie and then immediately L (Pl Centrale) to reach centre of **Bas-en-Basset** (17km, 462m) (accommodation, refreshments, camping, tourist office, station).

Bas-en-Basset (pop 4370) is a thriving market town. Its most notable building is the ruined Château Rochebaron, standing on a wooded hillside 150m above the town. The castle was built in the 12th century then gradually reinforced and extended to reach its maximum size in the 15th century. After its military significance declined it became a residential château, although poor living conditions rendered it unsuitable for this role and it was eventually abandoned. Nowadays it is a popular tourist attraction with regular events including archery contests and battle re-enactments.

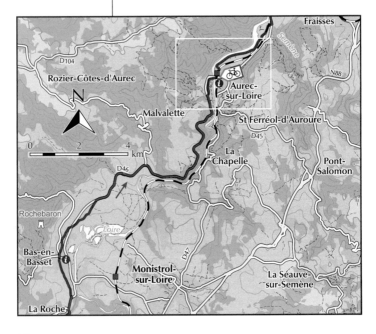

Go ahead into Rue du Commerce and fork R (Rte de la Loire). Continue into open country and go straight across main road (sp Os), passing refuse disposal site R. Pass through Os hamlet and cross an old iron bridge, then bear L, ascending gently to reach main road. Bear R (D46) and follow road for 9km, at first undulating through fields then descending through forest to the Loire. Ascend again before passing through forest 100m above the river, which is now in a deep gorge R.

Descend to reach beginning of Aurec-sur-Loire and turn R at roundabout (Rue de la Rivière). Pass bar and restaurant L and bear R between planters on footpath leading to recently renovated pedestrian suspension bridge over Loire. ▶ Cross river and railway to reach riverbank below centre of **Aurec-sur-Loire** (30km, 429m) (accommodation, refreshments, camping, tourist office, station). To visit town centre turn R (Rue de la Loire) and L steeply uphill (Rue des Puits) to reach Pl de l'Europe; alternatively, to continue onto Stage 5 turn L under modern road bridge.

Himalayan-style suspension bridge over the Loire at Aurec-sur-Loire

A sign on the footpath requests that cyclists dismount and walk bicycles across the bridge.

Aurec-sur-Loire is known for its award winning trompe l'oeil murals

Aurec-sur-Loire (pop 6130) was another medieval walled town, and a few remnants of the walls, gates and castle can be seen in the old town centre surrounding the church. The suspension bridge over the Loire was built in 1892 and was the main river crossing until it was replaced by the current road bridge in 1969. The deck was removed in 1981, but the pylons were left in position. In 2012 a new bridge deck was constructed and the renovated bridge reopened as a 'Himalayan-style' pedestrian-only crossing.

The most noticeable objects d'art in Aurec are eight huge trompe l'oeil murals depicting aspects of medieval life that have been painted on buildings around the town centre. In 2014 one of these murals, *Porte d'Aurec*, won the golden paintbrush – an international award for the world's best examples of public art.

STAGE 5

Aurec-sur-Loire to Feurs

Start	Aurec-sur-Loire, pedestrian bridge (429m)
Finish	Feurs, Pl du 11 Novembre (346m)
Distance	58.5km
Waymarking	Véloire V71, planned Aurec–Montrond then waymarked Montrond–Feurs

Between Aurec and St Just the Loire has carved a deep gorge through the last part of the volcanic mountains, across which a hydro-electric dam at Grangent has created a large lake, part of the Loire Gorges natural park. After first following the river for a short distance, this stage climbs through forest high above the gorge and then descends steeply to reach the Forez plain. Beyond St Rambert the route becomes completely flat as it crosses the river and uses quiet country lanes to reach Feurs.

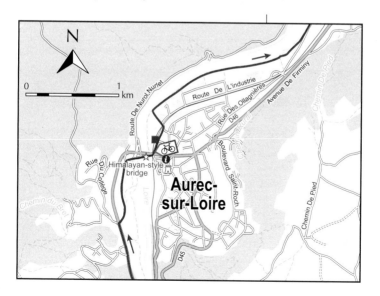

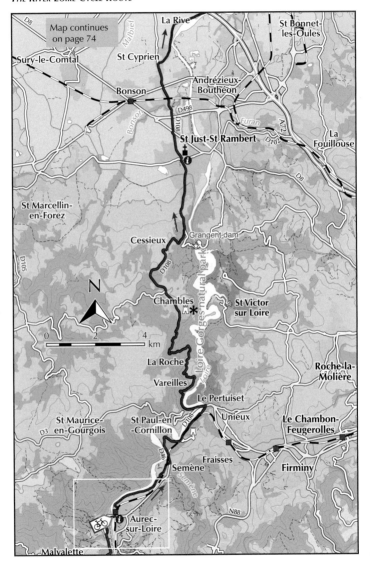

Map continues
on page 74

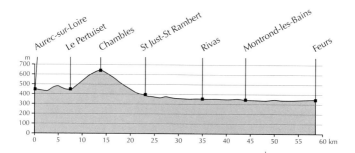

From the E end of Loire footbridge in **Aurec-sur-Loire**, follow Rue de la Loire N under road bridge. Continue past
station L into Rue des Cheminots then bear L (Rue de
l'Industrie) over railway level crossing. Immediately after
railway, fork L ahead (Rue de St Geneix) with MGPA factory R and follow gravel track to riverbank. Turn R along
riverbank, then where track turns R away from river, fork
L to continue beside river. Emerge beside boat landing quay L and continue ahead through two gravel car
parks (accommodation, refreshments). At end of second
car park, bear L onto road and cross bridge over river
Semène into **Semène** village (refreshments).

Follow road winding through village to reach floral roundabout decorated with bird boxes. Turn L (third
exit, D46, sp St Paul-en-Cornillon) and follow road
(Rte des Gorges) through two tunnels and along side of
gorge with Loire below L. Bear sharply R in **St Paul-en-
Cornillon** (now D108) and descend towards river with
basalt cliffs of old volcanic plug rising behind railway
viaduct R. ▶ Continue beside river to reach roundabout
in **Le Pertuiset** (7.5km, 436m) (accommodation, refreshments, camping).

Turn L (third exit, D3) to cross Loire on modern cable-
stay bridge. At end of bridge (refreshments) fork R (Rte
du Pertuiset, D108, sp Chambles) and begin climbing
through forest high above Loire gorge. Continue ascending round series of hairpins for 7km, passing through
hamlets of **Vareilles** (10km, 522m) (refreshments) and

St Paul-en-Cornillon
(pop 1360) is spread
over the basalt cliffs
of an old volcanic
plug, with an
11th-century château
sitting on the top.

Volcanic outcrop at St Paul-en-Cornillon

La Roche to reach **Chambles** (14.5km, 635m) (refreshments), which can be seen on hilltop ahead long before it is reached.

> The hilltop village of **Chambles** (pop 1020) is dominated by La Tour de Chambles, an 18m-tall medieval defensive tower that can be climbed using internal ladders for extensive views of the Loire Gorges natural park and its neighbouring volcanic hills.

Cycle through the village and descend for 8km, at first through fields to Laborie and then through forest to **Cessieux** (18.5km, 487m) (refreshments). Continue downhill into beginning of St Rambert. Enter town on Rte de Chambles. Continue over crossroads into Rue Gonyn, which leads to Pl Grenette. Turn R and L to leave square by opposite corner (Rue du 8 Mai). Turn R into attractive Rue Colombet-Solle, with many half-timbered houses, and immediately L through old gateway into cobbled courtyard of St Rambert priory in centre of **St Just-St Rambert** (22.5km, 390m) (refreshments, tourist office).

St Just and St Rambert (pop 15,000) are twin towns that merged in 1973. The attractive old centre of St Rambert west of the Loire has streets of half-timbered houses grouped around Prieuré St Rambert priory and Romanesque church – an ancient Benedictine monastery complex that housed the relics of St Rambert and became a centre for medieval pilgrimage.

Larger St Just, on the other side of the river, is an old industrial town that developed at the highest point of navigation on the Loire. From here barges carrying coal from the St Étienne coalfield were swept downriver by the current as far as Nantes. As there was no way of returning, these barges were used only once then broken up for firewood at their destination. Barge-building, dyeing, glass-making and metallurgical industries grew up around the town.

Continue ahead into Rue de Simian de Montchal and ahead again at crossroads (Rte de St Côme, D108). Go

Half-timbered houses in St Rambert

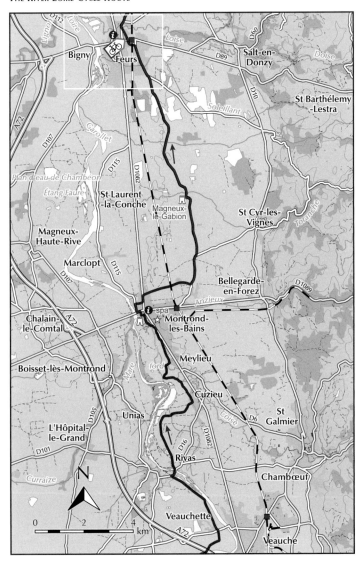

ahead at roundabout (second exit, D108, sp St Cyprien) to leave town. Pass over motorway and cross river Bonson by Pont du Diable bridge into edge of **Bonson** (accommodation, refreshments, station).

Continue ahead over railway crossing, then go ahead over roundabout (Rue de la Becque, second exit, D108, sp St Cyprien) into beginning of St Cyprien. Go ahead again over mini-roundabout (Rue des Bruyasses, second exit, D108, sp Craintilleux), using cycle lane R, then turn R beside house 1 (Rue du Tabot). Bear L at T-junction (Rue Germaine Robin) into centre of **St Cyprien** (27.5km, 373m) (refreshments).

Go ahead L at mini-roundabout (Rue Antoine Bufferne) then fork R (Rue des Balmes, sp cimetière) and follow this out of town into **La Rive** hamlet (accommodation). Continue along riverbank (Ch des Chambons) then pass under motorway and continue through fields to reach roundabout in **Veauchette** (31.5km, 356m) (refreshments).

Go ahead at roundabout (second exit, Rue du Vieux Bourg) and after 75m fork R (Ch de Malepine). Follow quiet road out of village into open country to reach T-junction. Turn R (Rte de Rivas, D101) and cross Loire to reach crossroads at beginning of **Rivas** (35km, 351m) (refreshments).

Turn L (Ch de la Vorzillière) then pass entrance to concrete factory R and fork R (sp La Vorzillière) on quiet road winding through fields to **Cuzieu** (38.5km, 350m) (refreshments). Turn L at crossroads (Rue de la Grande Bourgée) then follow road into open country, passing boules piste R, and bear L at T-junction. Continue winding through fields and turn R at next T-junction. Cross river Croise by seasonal ford and bear R into **Meylieu** (refreshments). ▶

A pedestrian bridge to the right of the road can be used if the river is high.

Immediately before first house on L, turn L on narrow gravel track behind houses (Ch de St Pierre), then at end of this track bear L on country lane (Ch d'Urfé). Continue straight ahead, avoiding turns to R and L, to emerge eventually beside main road. Cycle parallel to road for 75m, then bear L opposite casino (Rue du Vieux

Ruined Montrond castle is undergoing extensive renovations

Moulin) and turn L at T-junction (sp Château). Cross river Anzieux, then fork R (Promenade Marguerite d'Albon), passing well-preserved ruins of **Château de Montrond** L.

Go ahead over pedestrian bridge (crossing walkway along route of disused railway) and turn L (Rue Émile Dupayrat). Just before St Roch church L, turn R (Rue de Boissieu) and continue to T-junction in **Montrond-les-Bains** (44km, 349m) (accommodation, refreshments, tourist office, station).

> **Montrond-les-Bains** (pop 5300) grew up around a medieval castle that controlled a fording point over the Loire between Burgundy and Auvergne. The castle was destroyed by fire during the Revolution (1793) and subsequently fell into ruin. Since 1969 work has been undertaken to consolidate the remains and restore part of the building.
>
> In 1879 a mine shaft, being dug to seek coal, struck hot mineralised water 475m below the surface. The water gushed to a height of 7m and was named 'La Source Thermale du Geyser'. The

health-giving qualities of the water attracted visitors
and in 1938 the town – originally called Montrond
– was rechristened Montrond-les-Bains. The flow
of water declined eventually and in 1986 a new
deeper shaft was bored that increased both the flow
and temperature of the water. Subsequent development has seen new spas and a cultural and conference centre added to the town's tourist facilities.

Turn L onto main road (Ave du Pont) and R just
before Loire bridge (Rue de la Loire, D115, sp Marclopt).
Continue ahead at first road junction then turn R into
turning circle for school buses. Pass between schools L
and R, then fork R (Rue des Montagnes du Soir) to reach
crossroads. Turn L (Ave de la Route Bleue, D1082) then
first R (Rue de Ravatey, sp Complexe sportif Ravatey).
Continue ahead (Rue des Rotys), past fire station L, into
open country. Cross railway and continue through St
André-le-Puy (47km, 360m).

At end of village, turn L at T-junction (Rte de St-Cyr,
D16), then after 1.3km turn L (Rte de la Liégue, D112, sp
Feurs). Pass through Magneux le Gabion (51km, 357m)
and at end of hamlet bear R (Rte de Magneux, D112, sp
Feurs) continuing through fields. Road becomes Rte des
Places to reach beginning of Feurs. Turn L at T-junction
(D18, sp Feurs) then keep R at fork (Rte de Valeille). Pass
grain silos R and continue into Rue Marc Seguin, using
cycle lane R. Where cycle lane ends at crossroads, turn L
(Bvd Pasteur, sp Centre Ville) and go ahead over railway
crossing. Turn R (Rue Parmentier) to reach stage end at
crossroads beside war memorial in Pl du 11 Novembre
in **Feurs** (58.5km, 346m) (accommodation, refreshments,
camping, tourist office, cycle shop, station).

Feurs (pop 8250) was a Gallic settlement that the
Romans developed into a large town, some remains
of which can be seen near the post office. After the
Romans departed, the town went into a long period
of decline. In 1356, during the Hundred Years'
War, Feurs was enclosed by high walls and there

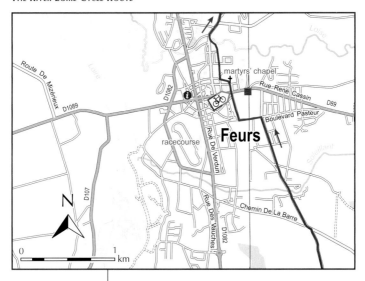

followed a period of prosperity as a small independent city-state that did not become part of France until 1534. The Reign of Terror and destruction that followed the Revolution left the town in a bad state. Eighty victims of the Terror are commemorated by the Martyrs' Chapel, a memorial in the form of a Greek temple built in 1826. After the Revolution the city walls were removed and a bridge built over the Loire to improve communications.

STAGE 6

Feurs to Roanne

Start	Feurs, Pl du 11 Novembre (346m)
Finish	Roanne, Port de Roanne (275m)
Distance	62.5km
Waymarking	Véloire V71

This stage starts by heading north on quiet country roads through agricultural country east of the Loire. After Balbigny the route becomes hillier as it climbs into the Monts de Beaujolais above the lake formed when Villerest dam was constructed across the Loire gorge in 1984. The lake is crossed at Bully port and the route undulates through hills on the west bank before following the river into Roanne.

From war memorial in **Feurs**, cycle N through Pl 11 du Novembre. At end, cross Rue de la Varenne and take cycle track into park immediately L of Martyrs' Chapel. ▶ Follow track winding through wooded parkland and emerge on road. Turn R (Rte de Civens, D107) past car park then continue ahead on dual carriageway (sp Civens). Immediately after sign for end of Feurs, fork L through Bellevue. At end of built-up area, continue

The Martyrs' Chapel, in Greek classical style, commemorates 80 victims of the Terror that followed the French Revolution.

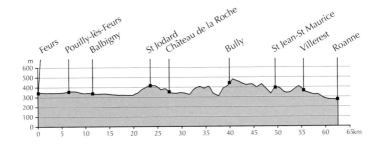

through fields to reach T-junction. Turn R over railway crossing and after 100m turn L on narrow road (Le Grand Chemin) winding through fields. Pass timber yard R then bear L at T-junction (Rue de la Libération, D10) into **Pouilly-lès-Feurs** (6.5km, 365m) (refreshments).

> **Pouilly-lès-Feurs** (pop 1220) is a small walled town that grew up around a 10th-century Clunaic priory with an 11th-century Romanesque church and the ruins of an ancient castle.

Go ahead L over crossroads (Rue de Cluny, D10, sp Balbigny) and cycle out of town. Turn L (sp Le Buis) beside modern white house onto quiet country road. Immediately before railway crossing, turn R (Ch de Chassagny) beside railway and continue through fields. Go ahead over mini-roundabout (Rue Jean-Claude Rhodamel) to reach larger roundabout on edge of Balbigny. Turn L (Rue C. Roche, third exit, sp Collège), then after 175m, opposite Collège Michel de Montaigne, turn R on gravel track between houses. Go ahead across road and cross stream, then bear R on road (Bvd de la Tuilerie) between industrial units. Fork R opposite station to reach T-junction in **Balbigny** (11.5km, 335m) (refreshments, station).

> In the early 19th century, **Balbigny** (pop 2900) was an important port on the Loire. Traditional Loire flat-bottomed barges carrying St Étienne coal downstream from St Rambert would stop here to change crews before continuing to Roanne. This ended abruptly in 1832, when one of the first railways in France opened between Andrézieux-Bouthéon and Roanne specifically to transport coal from the St Étienne coalfield.

Turn L (Rue du Four à Chaux) and immediately fork R (Rue de l'Industrie), past bus station L. At end of town, fork L following road beside railway L. In Lachat (accommodation), turn L through barriers onto bridge over

railway. Dog-leg L and R to cross main road then fork L
(Rte de Bernand, D56, sp Pinay) and follow this bearing L
in Bernand (refreshments). Pass Pralery L (camping) then
continue to reach Loire and pass under motorway bridge.
Continue beside river L, passing under two road bridges
and after second bridge (in La Digue) ascend round hairpin bend to reach **Pinay** (22km, 410m) (refreshments).

Turn L in village (Rue de la Croix de Mission, D56,
sp St Jodard) then descend out of village into small valley

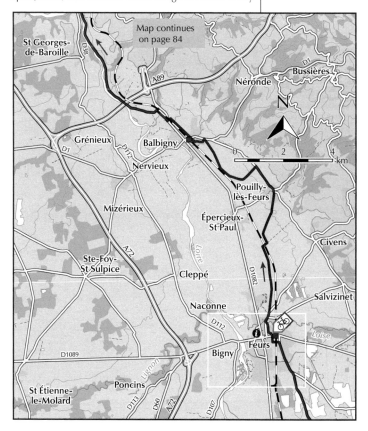

Map continues
on page 84

and climb back up other side to **St Jodard** (23.5km, 419m) (refreshments, station).

> **St Jodard** (pop 400) is dominated by the priory of the Community of St Jean, a devout and proselytising Catholic sect that was founded in Freiburg (Germany) in 1975 and opened a novitiate priory (where new members are taught and initiated into the order) in St Jodard in 1983. Over 4000 members of the order, many of whom spent seven years training at St Jodard, live in 91 priories in 21 countries. The community's strong proselytising methods, where new entrants are pressurised into giving up contact with their families and abandoning modern medical treatments, have been widely criticised within the Catholic Church.

If you visit the castle you can regain the route by following a track past the entrance and ascending to reach the road.

Cycle through village and descend through open country past station L. Cross railway and continue descending. Fork R at road junction (D56, sp Château de la Roche) then pass turn-off L that leads to **Château de la Roche** and soon pass above castle standing on rock in middle of Loire (27.5km, 333m) (refreshments). ◄

> The spectacularly positioned **Château de la Roche** was built between 1256 and 1291 on a rocky outcrop 30m above the Loire, and was used mostly as a toll castle to collect tolls from passing boats. Frequent flooding led to its abandonment in the 17th century. In the late 19th century the ruins were purchased by an industrialist from Roanne who restored it in Gothic style as a second home. When the Villerest dam was completed in 1984 the lake behind the dam surrounded the castle and left it isolated on an island. It was purchased by the local commune and remodelled in 1996 with an access causeway linking it to the riverbank.

Continue with view of Loire (actually Villerest lake) in gorge below L, descending to cross an arm of

lake. Ascend away from river past turn-off for campsite (refreshments, camping), then road undulates to reach triangular junction. Fork L (D45, sp Bully) and follow road steeply downhill to Pont de Presle bridge over narrow part of Villerest lake. Cross lake to Port de Bully (36.5km, 333m) (refreshments) and follow road (Rte du Pont de Presle, D45) winding first through forest then fields and ascending steadily to **Bully** (40km, 461m) (refreshments).

Continue ascending through village past church R to reach crossroads and turn R (Rte du Charizet, D203, sp St Jean-St Maurice). Follow winding road descending through forest then ascend into hilltop town of **St Jean-St Maurice-sur-Loire** (48.5km, 377m) (accommodation, refreshments).

Follow Rue de l'Union winding uphill through town then pass church R and turn R (Rte de la Bruyère, D203) undulating through fields to reach crossroads (52km, 359m). Turn R (Rte de St Sulpice, D18, sp Villerest) following road uphill to Les Hauts de Roy (refreshments) then descend to reach roundabout in **Villerest** (55.5km, 354m) (accommodation, refreshments, camping).

The spectacularly positioned Château de la Roche is surrounded by the waters of Villerest lake

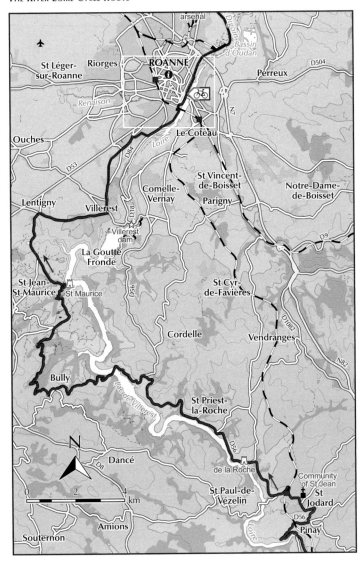

Plans to build the **Barrage de Villerest dam** were first mooted before 1914, intended to provide a municipal water supply for Paris. Land was purchased but the scheme was blocked by local objections. A revised plan in the 1930s to build a hydro-electric dam was abandoned because of the Second World War. By 1966 a new requirement had emerged: four nuclear power stations were proposed for construction beside the Loire and a means of controlling the flow of the river to provide a consistent supply of cooling water was needed. Added to this was a desire to provide flood protection at times of high river flow and irrigation at times of drought. As a result, when the dam was constructed between 1978 and 1984 it was built primarily for hydrological reasons with electricity generation as a secondary purpose. The finished dam is an attractive concrete crescent spanning the narrowest part of the gorge. The lake above the dam has seen a growth of tourist facilities both on the water and along its banks.

Turn L (Rue Jean Moulin, third exit, sp Villerest-Bourg) using cycle lane R. Go ahead over two roundabouts, then after second roundabout fork L (Ch Beauregard). Follow this downhill, going ahead over next roundabout (Rue de la Mirandole, sp Haite Garderie). Pass house 82 on L and turn R (Rue des Rives de Loire) downhill. Turn L at roundabout (second exit, still Rue des Rives de Loire) and go ahead over crossroads (Rue du Moulin À Vent Prolongé). Turn R at next crossroads beside house 113 (Rue du Commières) to reach riverbank at beginning of Roanne.

Turn L, using cycle track behind wooden railings R. Where railings end, bear R steeply downhill to riverside. Pass allotments L, then turn L on gravel track and bear R uphill to regain main road. Continue along flood dyke, then bear L before railway bridge to reach road (Rue du Rivage). Continue ahead to crossroads and turn R (Rue Hoche) under railway bridge then over river Renaison.

Fork R at traffic lights and continue under road bridge to reach large gravel-surfaced square in front of Port de Roanne canal basin in **Roanne** (62.5km, 275m) (accommodation, refreshments, tourist office, cycle shop, station).

ROANNE

Port de Roanne canal basin is the head of navigation in the Loire valley

The old centre of Roanne (urban pop 104,000) grew up around an 11th-century castle. As trade developed on the Loire the town expanded to encompass a riverside port at the highest bi-directional point of navigation on the river, which prospered as a trans-shipment point for goods traded between the Rhone and Loire basins. The construction of a canal and railways in the 1830s, and the development of textile production, enabled the city to thrive during the industrial revolution. The most significant industrial development occurred during the First World War (1917) when a huge arsenal (munitions factory) was built between Roanne and Mably, north of the city. Eventually employing 11,000 people, the arsenal grew into a small city with its own housing estates, transport facilities, power generation and water supply. Although much reduced in size, the factory is still active, nowadays producing tanks and armoured cars for the French military and for export. The most visited tourist attractions are in the old town and include the castle keep and dungeon, St Étienne church, half-timbered houses and ivy-clad buildings.

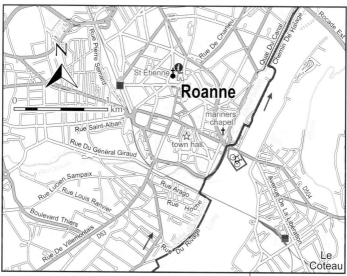

St Étienne church and medieval houses in Roanne

STAGE 7
Roanne to Digoin

Start	Roanne, Port de Roanne (275m)
Finish	Digoin, Sq de Gerolstein (239m)
Distance	58km
Waymarking	Véloire V71 Roanne–St Yan, none St Yan–Digoin

Leaving the volcanic mountains of the Massif Central behind, the Loire heads north into the Charolais region of southern Burgundy, famous for its iconic creamy white breed of cattle. This generally level stage uses voie vertes along a canal towpath and an old railway track to St Yan then a busy main road to reach Digoin, an important town on the French canal network. The busy road can be avoided by an 11km diversion.

From middle of gravel-surfaced square at S end of **Port de Roanne** canal basin follow unnamed road E then bear L (Quai de l'Ile) to pass along E side of canal basin. Follow road bearing R, then turn L (Quai du Commandant de Fourcauld) over small bridge and continue with Loire R to Pl Thiodet. Bear L before ultra-modern fire station then turn immediately R (Allée Jules Clerjon de Champagny) beside canal. Cycle under motorway bridge, then where canalside road turns R, fork L on cycle track beside canal. Pass former fortifications of Roanne Arsenal munitions factory on opposite bank. Follow towpath past **Cornillon** lock (9.5km) to reach road junction beside **Briennon** bridge (15km, 260m). ◄

To visit Briennon (accommodation, refreshments) turn L over bridge.

Turn R (D4) using cycle lane R and cross bridge over Loire. Immediately after bridge turn R (Rue du Port, one-way with contra-flow cycling permitted), then after 500m turn L on asphalt cycle track on voie verte along trackbed of disused railway through **Pouilly-sous-Charlieu** (16.5km, 263m) (accommodation, refreshments, camping). Go ahead over crossroads and pass old station R.

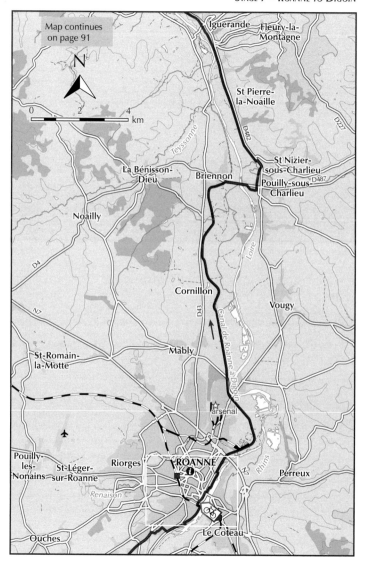

Map continues
on page 91

Iguerande

Fleury-la-
Montagne

St Pierre-
la-Noaille

St Nizier-
sous-Charlieu

Pouilly-sous-
Charlieu

La Bénisson-
Dieu

Briennon

Noailly

Cornillon

Vougy

Mably

St-Romain-
la-Motte

arsenal

Pouilly-
les-
Nonains

St-Léger-
sur-Roanne

Riorges

ROANNE

Perreux

Ouches

Le Coteau

*The voie verte
follows an old railway
from Pouilly-sous-
Charlieu to St Yan*

Cross river Sornin then fork L immediately before road bridge. Follow cycle track beside main road R for 350m, then dog-leg L and R to re-join course of disused railway and continue to **Iguerande** (23.5km, 260m) (accommodation, refreshments).

Continue on voie verte, at first parallel with main road then past Champceau hamlet and **St Martin-du-Lac**. Cross main road and continue on cycle track to reach T-junction. Turn R (Rte du Port d'Artaix) behind railings then after 60m turn L and bear R to reach site of old station on edge of **Marcigny** (33km, 249m) (accommodation, refreshments, tourist office, cycle shop).

The attractive little market town of **Marcigny** (pop 1750) was the site of an important women's priory founded by the Abbot of Cluny in 1054. The most notable remains are a defensive tower built between 1409 and 1419, and the priory mill. In 1266 a charter was granted for a weekly market and this still operates every Monday morning. Other attractions include a museum of horse-drawn vehicles and the Bourgogne du Sud gallery dedicated to the work of German artist Hartlib Rex (1936–2009), who lived his later years in Marcigny.

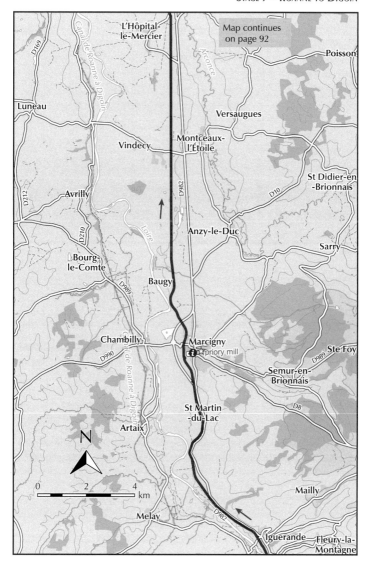

Map continues on page 92

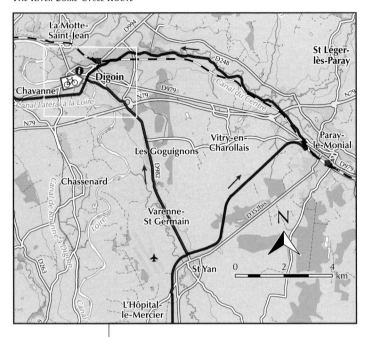

St Yan airfield
houses ENAC,
a college which
teaches instrument
flying techniques
to commercial
airline pilots.

From station site follow cycle track along railway trackbed out of town and over road bridge. Continue past hamlets of **Baugy** (accommodation), Réffy and La Villeneuve to reach site of former **Vindecy** station R (41.5km, 251m). Follow cycle track straight ahead for 5.5km then bear R beside D382. After 200m, turn L across road to re-join route of old railway and pass between La Plaine R and St Yan airfield L. ◄ Fork R beside car park, then cross river Arconce to reach road junction in **St Yan** (49km, 240m) (refreshments) and turn L (Rue Jules Ferry). Just before T-junction, turn L on cycle track and L again after 40m onto main road (Rte de Digoin, D982).

To avoid busy main road
D982 is a busy main road with heavy trucks and no cycle lane. To avoid this you could continue on V71 along the

old railway line to **Paray-le-Monial** then join EV6 and follow this along towpath of Canal du Centre to reach Digoin. This route is waymarked, level and cycle-friendly but adds 11km.

Continue through **Varenne-St Germain** (50.5km, 240m) (accommodation) then ascend through **Les Goguignons** (53.5km, 269m) and Tranche Gorge. Cross bridge over motorway then just before roundabout, turn L across road and join cycle track L of fourth exit (VC9, sp Digoin Stades). Continue downhill then fork L after 1km (Rue des Perruts). Pass Observa'Loire visitor centre L and cross bridge over canal Latéral à Loire to reach Sq de Gerolstein beside canal in **Digoin** (58km, 239m) (accommodation, refreshments, camping, tourist office, station).

The Digoin aqueduct over the Loire is an important link in the French canal system

93

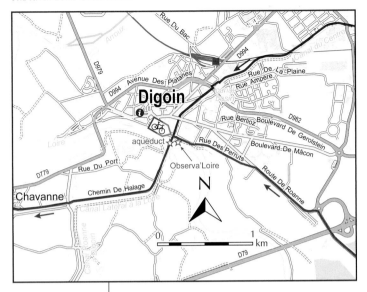

Digoin (pop 7750) is an important town on the French canal network, being the junction of three canals: Roanne à Digoin, Latéral à la Loire and Canal du Centre, which links the Loire with the Rhone/Saone basin. The Canal du Centre passes through the middle of town with extensive quays and wharfs then crosses the Loire by an aqueduct. The Observa'Loire visitor centre explains the history of the Loire and its canals.

STAGE 8

Digoin to Bourbon-Lancy

Start	Digoin, Sq de Gerolstein (239m)
Finish	Bourbon-Lancy, Plan d'Eau lake (227m)
Distance	31km
Waymarking	EV6

After Digoin the route follows EuroVelo EV6 mostly along dedicated asphalt cycle tracks. The first half is along the towpath of the canal Latéral à la Loire from Digoin to Diou; the route then crosses the Loire and follows a voie verte cycle track along a disused railway to reach the medieval walled town of Bourbon-Lancy. The stage is flat, although if you visit Bourbon-Lancy it is uphill at the end.

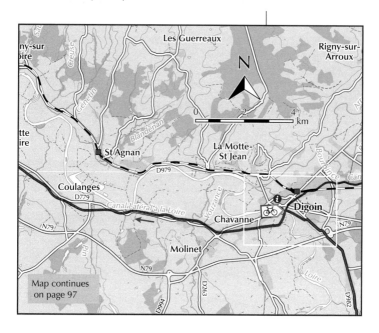

Map continues on page 97

The cycle route follows the towpath of canal Latéral à la Loire near Diou

Warning! Alongside each lock the surface changes to loose gravel designed to slow down cyclists.

To visit Diou (accommodation, refreshments, camping), continue ahead on the towpath for 1km.

From Sq de Gerolstein beside canal Latéral à la Loire in **Digoin**, follow Levée du Canal Latéral S down to towpath and continue ahead over Loire on Pont canal de Digoin aqueduct. Pass lock 1 (Digoin), then join road briefly and fork L to continue on towpath past **Chavanne** (2.5km, 230m) to reach **Coulanges** (10km, 228m) (refreshments). ◄ Continue along towpath past **Pierrefitte-sur-Loire** (14.5km, 226m) (accommodation, refreshments, camping).

After lock 5 (Putay), cycle track bears R off towpath onto parallel country road and then re-joins towpath at next bridge. Continue under railway bridge and after 150m bear R through gate away from towpath to reach road. ◄ Turn R over Loire into **Les Carrières** (20km, 218m).

Turn L just before T-junction up short slope, then fork L onto cycle track along course of old railway. Continue parallel with main road, then cross road and pass site of old station in **St Aubin-sur-Loire** (24.5km, 230m).

Château de St Aubin stands on a low rise north of the village. It was built (1771–1777) for Charles Gallois de la Tour to replace an older castle that stood on the banks of the Loire. Gallois de la Tour

STAGE 8 – DIGOIN TO BOURBON-LANCY

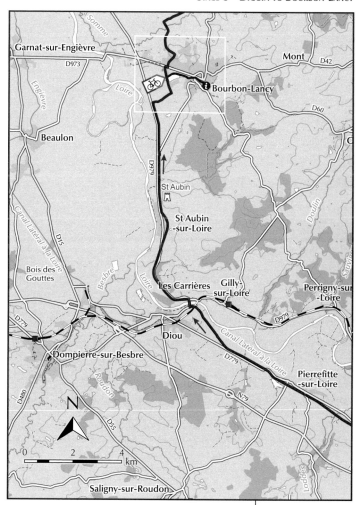

was imprisoned during the Revolution and died in 1802. His grandchildren gave the estate to the municipality of Bourbon-Lancy, who sold it to raise

97

money to build a hospital. Subsequently the château has changed hands many times. The current owner purchased it in 1999 and is in the process of restoring it to its former condition.

A newly built 6m palisade wall on the right prevents you from seeing the château's façade.

After village, route passes below Château de St Aubin then continues parallel with road. ◄ After 2km, track dog-legs R behind house then crosses side road and continues beside main road for further 2km to reach crossroads where there is car park L. Turn R (Rue du Fleury, sp Bourbon-Lancy par vélo route) and continue on country road between fields.

Turn L at T-junction (Rue des Eurimants) then go ahead over roundabout with tree in middle. Pass campsite and Plan d'eau lake (both R) to reach stage end beside Ibis Styles hotel in **Bourbon-Lancy** (31km, 227m).

To reach centre of Bourbon-Lancy
Turn R beside lake, passing hotel L and follow asphalt cycle track winding through parkland. Go ahead at

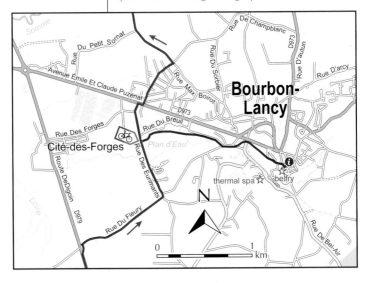

mini-roundabout (Rue de St Prix) passing car parks R. Just after end of car parks, turn L opposite swimming pool onto cycle track uphill through parkland (sp Centre Ville). Go ahead over crossroads and continue uphill on cycle track winding through parkland. Pass Château Puzenat R and emerge onto Rue des Bains. At end turn R (Rue du Commerce) to reach Pl de la Mairie in medieval centre of Bourbon-Lancy (2km off-route, 274m) (accommodation, refreshments, camping, tourist office, cycle shop).

Maison de Mme Sévigné in Bourbon-Lancy

Bourbon-Lancy (pop 4800) is a picturesque medieval walled hilltop town with a rather run-down thermal spa resort in the valley below. The old town has an ancient belfry, wooden houses and fortifications dating from 1495. It was a stronghold of the Bourbon family, who became the royal house of France in 1589.

STAGE 9
Bourbon-Lancy to Decize

Start	Bourbon-Lancy, Plan d'Eau lake (227m)
Finish	Decize, Pl St Just (195m)
Distance	46km
Waymarking	EV6

This stage, mostly away from the Loire, follows very quiet country roads. The route undulates through low hills in a pastoral landscape filled with Charolais cattle, but there are no long climbs. Near the end, the towpath of the Canal du Nivernais is joined to reach Decize.

From W end of Plan d'Eau lake in **Bourbon-Lancy**, follow Rue des Eurimants NW uphill to St Denis (refreshments). Turn R at T-junction then immediately L (Rue du Champblanc, sp Parc des Loisirs Robinson) still uphill to reach mini-roundabout by water tower. Turn L (Rue du Champ Aubé) then continue past Le Robinson leisure area R and cross river Somme. Turn R at next crossroads (sp Cronat) then bear L at T-junction and ascend gently. Road undulates through fields, passing through series of hamlets including La Place des Levées, to reach **Cronat** (16km, 228m) (accommodation, refreshments).

Turn L beside metal cross (Rue des Écoles, D196) to reach centre of village. Continue ahead (D979), passing hotel L, and after 100m where main road turns L, continue straight ahead (D196, sp Gannay). Pass church R and continue out of village, winding through fields for 3.5km to reach road junction where road ahead rises to cross Loire bridge. Before bridge, turn sharply R (D630, sp St Hilaire-Fontaine). ◀

To visit Gannay-sur-Loire (accommodation, refreshments, camping) continue ahead over bridge.

Cross river Cressonne and turn L (Ch de la Cressonne) on country lane winding through fields to reach Loire riverbank. Follow flood dyke for 400m with river L and

STAGE 9 – BOURBON-LANCY TO DECIZE

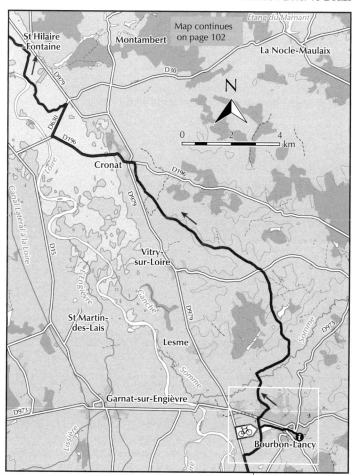

farmhouses R, then drop down R (sp St Hilaire-Fontaine) away from river through fields. Bear L at triangular junction (Rte de Thareau) and then continue ahead into **St Hilaire-Fontaine** (25km, 199m).

Pass church L and bear L (Rte de Tingeat) out of village, continuing to wind between fields to reach **Charrin** (28.5km, 197m) (accommodation, refreshments). At crossroads by war memorial, turn L (Rue du Quart) and immediately fork R (Rue de l'Église). Turn L at T-junction then bear R by wayside cross out of village. Turn R at triangular junction beside modern pumping station onto road along flood dyke and emerge beside Loire L. Turn R away from river (Rte des Gargolles), winding through fields for another 2.5km.

Turn L at junction, running below wooded hillside R, then ascend steeply and bear R (Ch de la Motte) to reach T-junction. Turn L (Rue de la Chaume) and R at next T-junction (Rue des Sarrasins) to reach main road

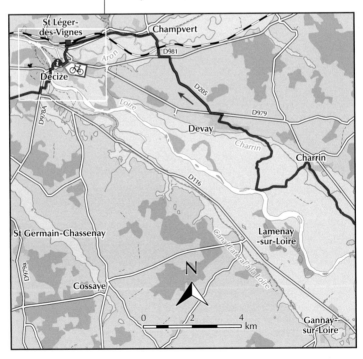

in middle of **Devay** (36km, 235m) (accommodation, refreshments).

Turn L on main road (D979) using cycle lane R. Just before end of village, turn R (D205, sp Champvert). Pass through Les Brosses hamlet to reach T-junction with another main road. Turn L (D981) on cycle lane R. Where cycle lane ends, turn R (D205, sp Canal du Nivernais) and continue through Beauregard hamlet. Cross railway and river Aron and bear L past **Champvert** lock R onto towpath of Canal du Nivernais (41.5km, 192m).

Continue on towpath under railway and road bridges and past large rubber products factory on opposite bank. Pass lock 34, then continue on towpath for 600m. Pass under next bridge then turn sharply L up to road. Turn R (Ave du 14 Juillet, D981, sp Decize) then cross Aron and go ahead on one-way system. Turn R at crossroads (D978A) and cross bridge over Vieille Loire old arm of river to reach end of stage in Pl St Just at beginning of **Decize** (46km, 195m) (accommodation, refreshments, camping, tourist office, station).

Bridge over Vieille Loire at Decize

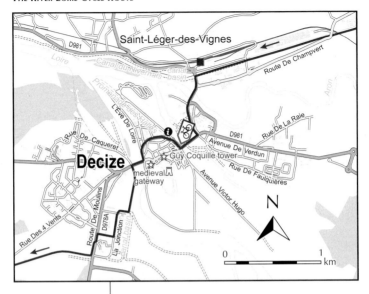

Decize (pop 5275) developed around an 11th-century castle on a rocky island between two arms of the Loire. As the eastern arm (Vieille Loire) has been blocked off upstream of Decize, the town now sits on a peninsula. Remains of medieval fortifications include ruins of the castle and its dungeons, parts of the moated city walls, watchtowers and la Porte du Marquis d'Ancre – a medieval city gate with a drawbridge. The parish church contains the relics of St Aré, a fifth-century bishop of Nevers. A local myth about his death describes his body being placed on a boat to float down the Loire. To everyone's surprise the boat floated 33km upstream to Decize, where it came to rest and the saint was buried on the site of an ancient Gallo-Roman temple. This has been incorporated within a crypt under the church.

During the industrial revolution the town became an important navigational centre at the junction of two canals.

STAGE 10

Decize to Nevers

Start	Decize, Pl St Just (195m)
Finish	Verville lock (Nevers turn-off) (176m)
Distance	34km (plus 4km into Nevers)
Waymarking	EV6

A completely level stage that follows the towpath of the canal Latéral à la Loire from Decize port to Verville lock, from where another towpath provides a link with the city of Nevers. No villages are passed through and facilities are limited.

From W end of bridge over Vieille Loire in **Decize**, follow Quai de Loire NW to reach roundabout. Fork L (D978A, second exit), passing car parks R, and follow road bearing L to reach Loire. Turn R across bridge over river. Immediately after bridge, turn L beside river (Levée de la

Fleury lock on canal Latéral à la Loire

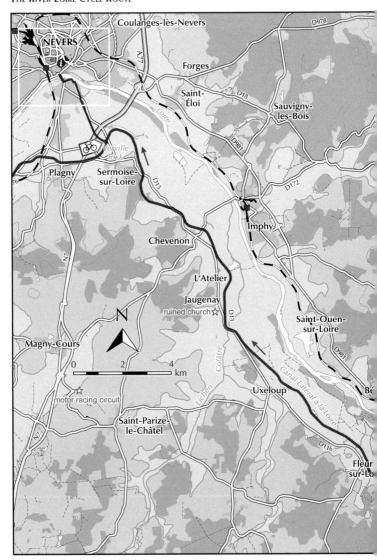

Jonction) and follow flood dyke to reach lock at entrance to canal Latéral à la Loire.

Turn R away from river and follow road bearing L to reach mini-roundabout. Continue ahead (second exit), passing hospital R, and turn R (Rue de la Jonction) passing between hospital and apartment buildings. Turn L at T-junction (D978A) past supermarket R and bear R onto red asphalt cycle track. Follow this to reach canal and bear R along towpath beside canal. Continue past **Avril-sur-Loire** (10km, 187m) R and **Fleury-sur-Loire** (14km, 184m) L (refreshments).

Follow towpath past **Uxeloup** L (18.5km, 183m) and continue to reach **Jaugenay** lock (23km, 179m).

The ruined former parish **church of St Étienne** in Jaugenay stands incongruously in a farmyard. The size of the building testifies to a much larger congregation in centuries gone by. After being badly damaged during the Revolution it was not repaired, and served as a barn for many years. Since the ruin was classified as a listed monument, some work has been done to conserve it.

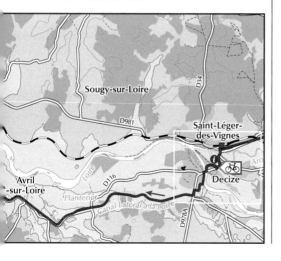

Continue along towpath past **L'Atelier** and **Chevenon** (27km, 178m) (refreshments, camping) to reach **Verville lock** (34km, 176m), where stage ends beside branch canal linking canal Latéral with Nevers. To continue onto Stage 11, cross lock and follow towpath W beside canal Latéral à la Loire.

To visit Nevers

Turn R alongside Embranchement de Nevers canal and follow towpath under motorway bridge. Drop down L under bridge at beginning of Nevers port, then continue beside canal basin L. Cycle through barrier, passing disused swimming pool complex L, then bear L on road over closed entrance to canal. Turn R on rough track along top of flood dyke passing campsite below R, then bear R to reach main road. Turn R (D907) on bridge over Loire to reach **Nevers** (4km from Verville lock) (accommodation, refreshments, camping, tourist office, cycle shop, station).

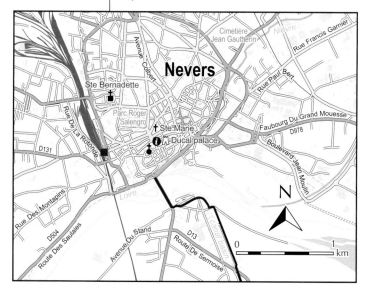

NEVERS

Nevers (urban pop 57,000) sits on the Butte, a low hill on the north bank of the Loire. Originally a Gallic settlement, it became a Roman town and then the site of a bishopric at the end of the fifth century. Narrow winding

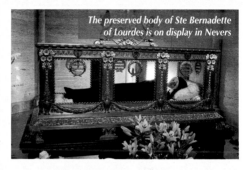

The preserved body of Ste Bernadette of Lourdes is on display in Nevers

streets lead from the riverside to the cathedral – really two churches in one, with two choirs, one Romanesque and one Gothic. The building is a mix of ancient and modern, the ancient being a sixth-century baptistery while modernity is represented by a collection of 20th-century stained-glass windows by contemporary artists. Other notable buildings include the former ducal palace, which was built in the 15th century as home for the Duke of the Nivernais and is now municipally owned.

The Hermitage Ste Bernadette contains the embalmed and well-preserved body of Ste Bernadette of Lourdes, resting peacefully in a glass and bronze case. Bernadette Soubirous (1844–1879) was a poor girl who, aged 14, entered a convent run by nuns from Nevers in Lourdes (southwest France) to learn to read and write. One day while collecting firewood in a grotto she had a vision of the Virgin Mary, and this visitation recurred on 17 further occasions. Pilgrims were drawn to the site by stories of healing, and Lourdes has become one of Europe's most visited pilgrimage destinations. In order to fulfil her religious calling, in 1866 Bernadette moved to the mother religious house in Nevers, where she lived a humble and secluded life. After she died her body was preserved and has been on display since 1925. She was canonised in 1933.

Nevers has two claims to worldwide fame outside the city: the forests to the east are cultivated to produce Nevers white oak, which is regarded as the world's supreme material for wine barrel cooperage; and south of the city is Magny Cours motor racing circuit, formerly the venue of the French Grand Prix.

STAGE 11

Nevers to La Charité-sur-Loire

Start	Verville lock (Nevers turn-off) (176m)
Finish	La Charité-sur-Loire bridge (156m)
Distance	40km (plus 4km from Nevers)
Waymarking	EV6 to Bec d'Allier, then Loire à Vélo

This is another completely flat stage, following cycle tracks along a mix of canal towpaths and protective flood dykes. Waymarking for the Loire à Vélo cycle route starts opposite the confluence of the river Allier at Bec d'Allier. Few settlements are passed and there are very few services.

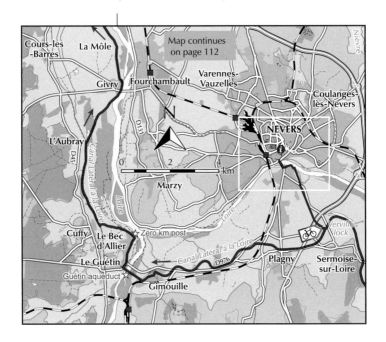

From **Verville lock** follow towpath of canal Latéral à la Loire SW, soon passing **Plagny** (2km, 177m) (refreshments) and Challuy (accommodation), both L. Continue past small Château du Marais behind trees R to reach bridge over canal at **Gimouille** (8.5km, 180m) (refreshments).

Turn L over canal and continue to reach mini-roundabout. Bear R (first exit, Rue du Pont Canal) then go ahead over staggered crossroads and continue along road parallel with quayside past old metal crane R. Turn R at end of quay and fork R over bridge, then turn L to continue along towpath on opposite bank. Follow canal across **Guétin aqueduct** over river Allier. Pass lock at end of aqueduct to reach road (D976) in **Le Guétin** (10.5km, 172m) (accommodation, refreshments).

The Guétin aqueduct passes high over the river Allier

111

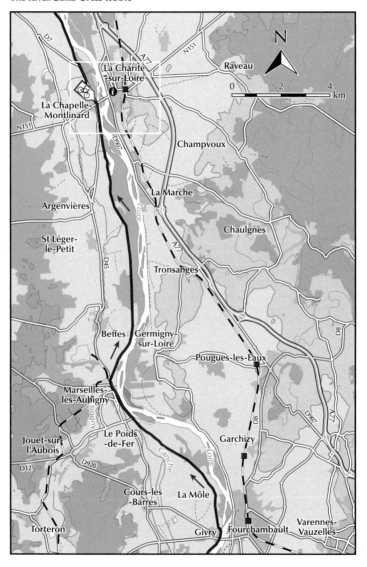

Cross road and turn R on service road L (Rue des Écluses, becoming Rue des Pêcheurs), passing beside roundabout R. Bear L (Allée du Déversoir) along flood dyke into **Le Bec d'Allier** (accommodation). Pass confluence of Loire and Allier and follow road bearing L (Levée du Bec d'Allier) along flood dyke. ▸ Just before no through road sign at end of village, fork L off flood dyke on narrow road (Rue de la Chaume).

Follow road winding through fields to reach canal and turn R along towpath. Continue for 3.5km past **L'Aubray** lock then turn R on country road along flood dyke (Levée des Joigneaux). Emerge beside Loire then drop down R to pass under end of Fourchambault bridge in **Givry** (19.5km, 166m) (refreshments). ▸

> Beside the track opposite the confluence is a metal post with the 'zero km' marker for Loire à Vélo cycle route.

> To visit Fourchambault (accommodation, refreshments, camping, station), turn R across the river.

> The industrial town of **Fourchambault** (pop 4200) grew up from 1821 with the construction of an iron works using the latest technology imported from Britain. Production increased rapidly and the furnaces were soon employing 4000 workers. Output was mostly iron rails and bridge components for the rapidly expanding French railway and canal systems. Other furnaces and foundries were opened and by 1854 the city was the largest French producer of iron. This golden age of Fourchambault iron lasted until 1883, after which strong competition from Lorraine caused rapid decline followed by closure of the furnaces in 1901. A long period of stagnation with high levels of unemployment and poverty continued until after the Second World War. During the 1950s Vespa scooters were produced in the town, and later Iveco and Renault produced trucks here. However, these factories have now closed and industrial decline has reappeared.

Continue ahead beside river (Levée de la Loire) and cross branch canal at Givry lock. Continue ahead on cycle track along top of flood dyke. Pass hamlet of **La Môle** L (21.5km, 165m) and continue ahead, now on

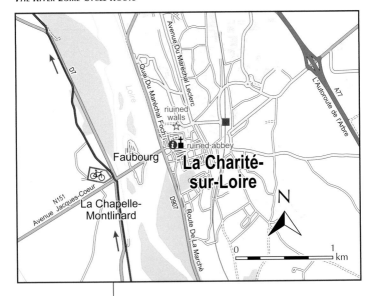

quiet road (Levée de la Môle) along flood dyke. Where road ends, continue ahead on cycle track for 2.5km to emerge on road through **Le Poids-de-Fer** hamlet (refreshments) where there is a short stretch of cycle track R. Continue through Port Conscience to reach **Marseilles-lès-Aubigny** (27.5km, 165m) (accommodation, refreshments), where there is another short cycle track R.

Opposite house 7, turn sharply L uphill to reach canal and sharply R before canal bridge to re-join towpath. Pass Aubois lock and go ahead over crossroads, then after 250m turn R across road onto minor road along flood dyke. Where road ends, continue on cycle track for 11km, with mostly fields L and riparian woodland R, to reach end of bridge over Loire in **La Chapelle-Montlinard** (40km, 156m) (accommodation, refreshments) opposite medieval town of **La Charité-sur-Loire** (accommodation, refreshments, camping, tourist office, station). ◀

To visit La Charité-sur-Loire, turn R over the bridge.

LA CHARITÉ-SUR-LOIRE

Parts of the ruined Clunaic abbey at La Charité-sur-Loire have been restored

La Charité-sur-Loire (pop 4800) developed around an important 11th-century Clunaic abbey built beside an early fording point of the Loire. When completed, the 12th-century abbey church of Notre-Dame was the second largest church in Christendom after its parent church at Cluny. Devastated by fire in 1559, the abbey and church were only partly rebuilt, the restored church being 40 per cent of its original size, although remnants of the unrestored part can be seen on the façade of the tourist office. During the Revolution the monks were expelled and the abbey building sold for use by tradesmen and as housing. The church continued in use and became one of France's first listed historic buildings. Since 2001 a huge project has been underway to restore the abbey, and the building is slowly regaining its former glory.

Soon after the abbey had been constructed, defensive fortifications were constructed around the town. Parts of these still stand, having been swallowed up by the town as it grew. The old part of the town within the walls is well preserved, with many narrow lanes and artisans' buildings. The monks constructed the stone bridge over the Loire in 1520 and it remains one of the oldest and most attractive bridges over the river. One part of the town, known as Faubourg, was constructed on a rocky island in the river.

In addition to tourists visiting the town to see the medieval abbey and restored buildings, La Charité has become known as the French book town, with many second-hand and antiquarian bookshops supported by a number of book fairs and festivals.

STAGE 12
La Charité-sur-Loire to Sancerre

Start	La Charité-sur-Loire bridge (156m)
Finish	St Thibault bridge (Sancerre) (147m)
Distance	24km (26.5km to Sancerre)
Waymarking	Loire à Vélo

Between Pouilly-sur-Loire and Sancerre the Loire has cut through a chalk ridge. This short, level stage, almost entirely along the top of the Loire flood dyke, follows the river through this gap. No towns or villages of any significance are passed. The stage ends below the medieval wine-producing village of Sancerre. An optional steep 150m climb provides access to the village.

From W end of bridge over Loire in **La Chapelle-Montlinard**, continue N on quiet road (Ch du Pont de la Batte) below flood dyke R. Follow this, winding through area of scattered housing before returning to flood dyke. Continue beside road on flood dyke (cycle track L), then where cycle track ends, cross main road and follow side road (sp Passy) with riparian woodland R to reach **Passy** (2.5km, 153m).

Where road ends, continue ahead on cycle track beside river then follow this along flood dyke away from river, winding through forest, field and scrub for 10km to reach T-junction at beginning of **Les Vallées** (13km, 152m).

Turn R into village and fork R, then continue ahead at crossroads (Rte des Rampes) out of village. ◀ Follow quiet road along flood dyke. Where this turns away from river, continue ahead on cycle track along riverbank. Where asphalt ends, turn L past lagoon R. Cross small bridge, then bear R to continue on cycle track. Turn R between fields and continue to reach turn-off L leading to Sancerre. Unless you are planning to visit Sancerre (see below) continue ahead, crossing wooden bridge and bearing R on

Turning R at the crossroads leads over the Loire to the wine-producing village of Pouilly-sur-Loire (accommodation, refreshments, camping, tourist office, station.

cycle track. Emerge onto road (Quai de Loire Hervé Mhun) and follow this to reach Loire. Continue to end of stage beside Loire bridge in **St Thibault** (24m, 147km) (accommodation, refreshments, tourist office).

To visit Sancerre

To visit wine-producing village of Sancerre, which sits on hilltop 2km W of route, turn L (sp Ménétréol) at turn-off described above. At road junction, where there are recycling bins L, turn R (Rte des Aubelles, sp Ménétréol). Cross canal bridge and main road into Rue de l'Église in **Ménétréol-sous-Sancerre** (150m) (accommodation, refreshments). Turn first R on narrow road (Rue Basse) between houses. At offset crossroads go L ahead (Rue de la Quintaine) and continue onto Rte de Sancerre (D920). Follow this as it winds uphill through vineyards round

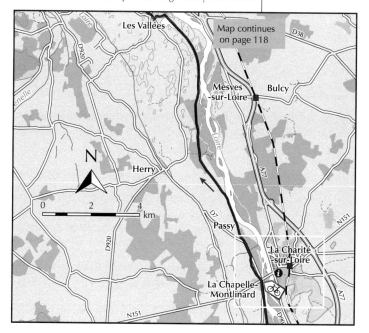

Map continues on page 118

Vineyards surround the hilltop town of Sancerre

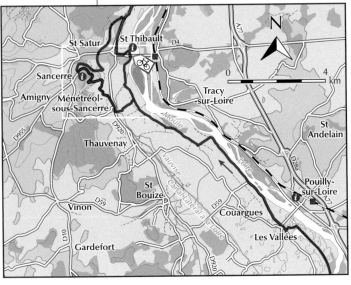

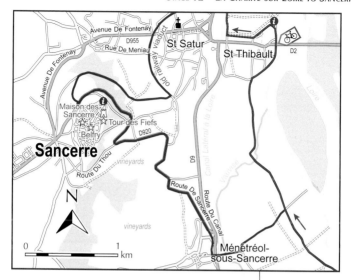

series of hairpins, becoming Rte de la Charité, to reach
entrance to **Sancerre** R at top of hill (4.5km from turn-off,
274m) (accommodation, refreshments, tourist office).

SANCERRE

The village of Sancerre (pop 1400) grew up around a medieval castle on
top of a 312m chalk hill, with ramparts to defend the city. These fortifications were strong enough to withstand two English sieges during the
Hundred Years' War. A Huguenot (Protestant) town during the Wars of
Religion, it was captured by Catholic forces after an eight-month siege
(1572–1573), the last time *trébuchets* (slings) were used in European war-
fare. After this defeat the castle and much of the walls were demolished
and there was an exodus of Protestant merchants and traders, leading to
a period of economic decline. The village today is a maze of little streets,
with many surviving medieval buildings. The Belfry of St Jean is a 16th-
century tower built by Huguenot merchants, while the Tour des Fiefs is the
only remaining tower of the old castle.

The Maison des Sancerre is dedicated to promoting Sancerre wine

Modern-day Sancerre is dominated by the wine industry. Prior to the 19th-century phylloxera devastation, Sancerre produced wine from pineau grapes. Replanting was mostly with sauvignon blanc, which produces an appellation contrôlée crisp white wine that is good with seafood and shellfish. Some pinot noir is also grown, mostly for local consumption. The 14th-century Maison des Sancerre houses a wine exhibition.

STAGE 13

Sancerre to Briare

Start	St Thibault bridge (Sancerre) (147m)
Finish	Briare, Pont du Port (134m)
Distance	43km (45.5km from Sancerre)
Waymarking	Loire à Vélo

This is a level stage following a mix of canal towpaths and cycle tracks along flood dykes and quiet country roads. It ends in the important canal hub of Briare.

Route from Sancerre

If you have visited **Sancerre** you can re-join the route by continuing ahead from entrance to town (Ave Nationale, D920) downhill to roundabout. Turn sharply R (Ave Honoré de Balzac, sp Le Feeling), continuing downhill through vineyards to reach T-junction. Turn L (sp Bannay) on road along course of old railway. Fork R at road junction to pass above edge of **St Satur** (accommodation, refreshments, camping) and continue over old railway viaduct. Go ahead at crossroads onto cycle track. Continue ahead to reach complicated path junction. Bear L and turn sharply R on track between vineyards, descending steeply to T-junction. Turn R under railway bridge and continue across main road and over canal bridge. Turn L along towpath to re-join main route (4.5km from Sancerre).

Main route

From W end of Loire bridge in **St Thibault**, cycle N beside Loire (Quai de Loire). Pass small red-brick tower on riverbank and fork L (Rue du Canal de Jonction) away from river alongside canal basin. Where road turns away from canal, fork R along canalside, passing Résidence St Pierre

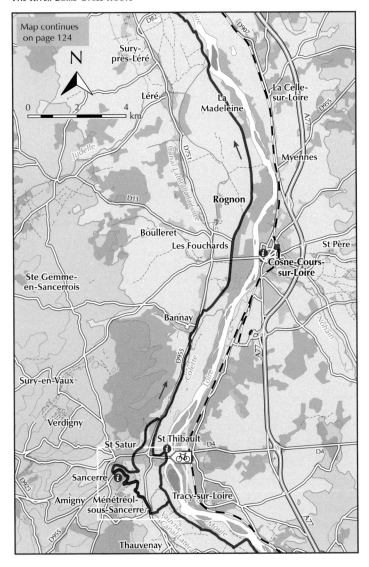

Map continues
on page 124

N

0   2   4
km

Sury-
près-Léré

Léré

La
Madeleine

La Celle-
sur-Loire

Myennes

Rognon

Boulleret

Les Fouchards

St Père

Cosne-Cours-
sur-Loire

Ste Gemme-
en-Sancerrois

Bannay

Sury-en-Vaux

Verdigny

St Satur   St Thibault

Sancerre

Amigny   Ménétréol-
sous-Sancerre

Tracy-sur-Loire

Thauvenay

L. Turn R across bridge over entrance to canal basin and where asphalt ends, drop down L onto cycle track beside canal Latéral à la Loire, passing junction with alternate route from Sancerre at first bridge.

Combined route continues
After 5km, turn L on bridge over canal and bear R. Cross main road and continue on cycle track L of road. Where this ends, turn L into **Bannay** (6km, 149m) (accommodation, refreshments).

Bear R (Rue de l'Église) through village, passing church R. Continue downhill on Rue du Puits d'Amour. Cross main road and drop down R onto cycle track along canal towpath. Turn R across canal at bridge over Bannay lock and L along opposite bank. Pass under railway bridge and bear R away from canal on cycle track along top of flood dyke to reach crossroads on edge of **Les Fouchards** (10km, 144m). ▸

Continue ahead (D13), soon joining cycle track L of road. Where road turns L, cross road and continue ahead (C1, sp Rognon) on quiet road along flood dyke with riparian woodland R, passing **Rognon** L (12.5km, 140m).

Continue on flood dyke past La Motte and **La Madeleine** hamlets, both L. Where road comes close to Loire and crosses small bridge over sidestream, bear R onto cycle track beside river. After 1.5km, by cyclist rest area L, follow road bearing L then turn R (sp La Fortay) on cycle track through fields directly towards power station.

Bear L and R alongside woods L and continue beside small lake. Bear L alongside security fence and flood dyke surrounding **Belleville nuclear power station**. Where road bears away L, fork R on cycle track parallel with fence. Emerge beside main road (D82) and continue along L side of employees' car park behind wooden railings.

Just before power station entrance, turn L across main road onto side road beside Maison de Loire du Cher R. Follow road over canal, then turn immediately R through maze of Jardins du Savoir. At end of maze, bear R

To visit Cosne-Cours-sur-Loire (accommodation, refreshments, camping, tourist office) turn R at crossroads and cross Loire bridge.

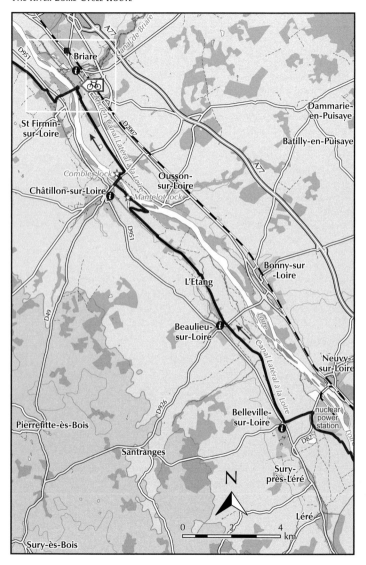

and continue along grass towpath beside canal for 300m, passing **Belleville-sur-Loire** (24km, 139m) (accommodation, refreshments, camping, tourist office).

At next bridge, turn R across canal and L along asphalt towpath on opposite bank. Continue past Maimbray lock to **Beaulieu-sur-Loire** (29km, 138m) (accommodation, refreshments, tourist office).

Pass under bridge and follow towpath to **L'Etang** (31km, 135m). Turn L over bridge across Châtillon branch canal then turn R before second bridge on towpath beside canal Latéral à la Loire. Pass under next bridge and turn R by lock at second bridge back over Châtillon branch. Turn L on gravel track along flood dyke beside Châtillon canal to reach crossing of tracks. Turn R, away from canal, on road winding through woods, and turn sharply L along flood dyke beside Loire R. Emerge on cobbled track and follow this over

Flower-bedecked Châtillon lock where the canal Latéral à la Loire reaches the Loire

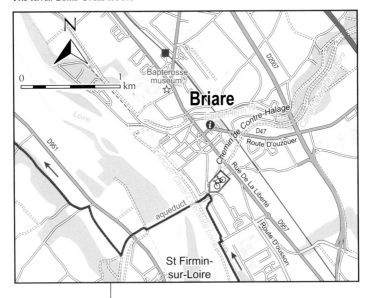

D50 is a busy
main road with
no cycle lane.

Mantelot lock (37km, 129m) (accommodation, refreshments, tourist office in Châtillon) at entrance from Loire to Châtillon canal.

Turn R alongside lock and bear L on gravel track beside Loire. Turn R to cross Loire on road (D50) over multi-stage suspension bridge. ◄ Immediately over bridge, turn R on cycle track dropping down to riverside and turn sharply R back under bridge. Continue over **Combles lock** (refreshments, camping) and turn R beside canal.

Follow gravel cycle track, bearing L beside canal pound and passing two bridges to reach T-junction. Turn R over canal on third bridge (Pont des Vignes) then L along opposite bank. Bear R uphill to reach road and turn L over Pont du Port bridge, where stage ends beside entrance to canal basin in **Briare** (43km, 134m) (accommodation, refreshments, camping, tourist office, station).

BRIARE

Briare (pop 5200) is positioned at the junction of two important canals and the Loire. The canal Henri IV, one of the first canals in France, was dug between 1604 and 1642 to connect the Loire and Seine basins and enable through-navigation between central France and Paris. The canal Latéral à la Loire was built 200 years later (1822) as part of a scheme to connect the Loire and Rhone basins, thus connecting central and southern France. The connection between these canals originally required haulage across the Loire; this proved difficult and unreliable, so in 1896 a new canal was built between the systems. This crosses the river on a 662m aqueduct, the longest in Europe at the time. Both canals have their own basins, locks and entrances to the Loire, with the town centre occupying the area between them. The canal systems enabled Briare to develop industrially. The most well-known industry was the production of earthenware, glass and enamel tiles and beads for use in mosaics. The Bapterosses factory still produces mosaics and its museum can be visited. Many of the town's churches and buildings are decorated with mosaics from this factory.

Canal bridge in Briare garlanded with flowers

STAGE 14
Briare to Sully-sur-Loire

Start	Briare, Pont du Port (134m)
Finish	Sully-sur-Loire, château (111m)
Distance	40.5km
Waymarking	Loire à Vélo

A mostly flat stage with a few gentle undulations that uses quiet country roads, cycle tracks along flood dykes and surfaced field paths. All of the villages passed have services and there are also remote farms that offer overnight accommodation.

From N side of Pont du Port canal bridge in **Briare**, cycle SW along towpath beside canal Latéral à la Loire across 662m-long pont-canal aqueduct over Loire. At end of aqueduct bear R away from towpath and then L, dropping down to crossroads. Go ahead (Rue du Canal) and after 250m turn sharply R on cycle track.

At T-junction, turn L on quiet road and after 75m fork R. After further 140m, fork R again onto gravel cycle track. Follow this between wooded hillside L and fields R, going ahead over two crossroads to reach T-junction. Turn L (Rue du Pont d'Ozion), ascending into **St Brisson-sur-Loire** (5.5km, 153m) (accommodation, refreshments).

At beginning of village, turn R (Rue de l'Église), passing church R. Continue ahead to château entrance and turn L (Rue du Château). At end bear L onto main road (Rue de Gien, D52) and turn R (Rue d'Enfert). Fork R (Rue de la Garenne) by roadside cross and at end continue ahead on cycle track through fields. Turn R downhill at T-junction (Ch des Chaussons) and L uphill at next T-junction (Rue des Vignes). Fork R (Rue de la Gratinère) and continue ahead at offset crossroads (Rue des Fontaines). Bear L to reach crossroads in middle of **St Martin-sur-Ocre** (8km, 137m) (refreshments).

Continue ahead on Rue des Grandes Vignes to reach crossroads. Turn R (Rte de la Californie, sp Gien) to leave village and continue winding through fields. Opposite house 146, fork R on gravel track (Impasse de la Californie). ▶ Pass under road bridge and turn L beside road.

This turn is easy to miss.

At next junction turn R, passing water tower L, and R again (Rue Cunion) into beginning of Gien. At end, cross main road and turn L on cycle track beside Loire. At end of cycle track, continue on road to reach roundabout at end of bridge over Loire in **Gien** (12.5km, 123m) (accommodation, refreshments, camping, tourist office, station). ▶

To visit Gien, turn R over the bridge.

GIEN

The view of Gien (pop 13,750) across the Loire is dominated by two huge buildings. The castle of Anne de Beaujeu was built at the end of the 15th century, incorporating remnants of an older fortification. Anne de Beaujeu was the eldest daughter of Louis XI; she became regent of France when her father died in 1483 and ruled the country until her younger brother was old enough to ascend the throne. This brick-built castle, which is noted for the patterning of its façade, became municipal property in 1823 and nowadays houses a museum of hunting. The other dominant structure is a church dedicated to Ste Jeanne d'Arc, who visited the town on a number of occasions.

Anne de Beaujeu's castle stands above Gien bridge

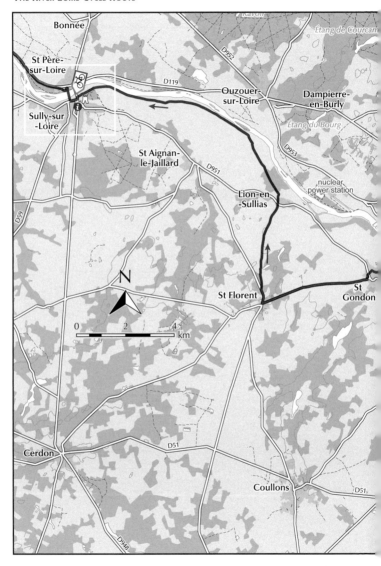

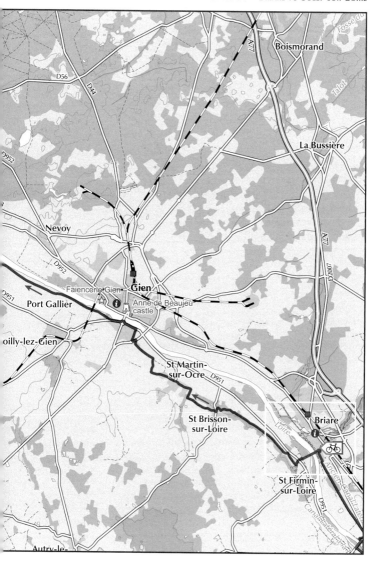

Boismorand

La Bussière

D56

D44

A77

D952

D2007

Nevoy

D952

D951

Faïencerie Gien

Port Gallier

Gien

Anne de Beaujeu castle

oilly-lez-Gien

St Martin-sur-Ocre

D951

St Brisson-sur-Loire

Loire

Briare

St Firmin-sur-Loire

D951

Autry-le-

Fossé du

Talot

Faïencerie Gien produced tableware for many French noble families

Originally built as a late Gothic church in the 15th century, all apart from the tower was destroyed by German bombing in 1940. After the war it was rebuilt in Romanesque style using brick as the principal material.

In June 1940, after German troops had invaded northern France, their air force attacked bridges over the Loire to prevent the French army from retreating south. The bombing of Gien was particularly severe and a fire started by the bombing destroyed most of the town, including churches, public buildings and 668 homes. The town was rebuilt in the 1950s, although a number of ruins have been preserved as a memorial to this destruction. The earthenware producer Faïencerie Gien, which was founded in 1821 by Englishman Thomas Hall, has grown to become one of the world's highest-quality glazed earthenware producers. The company has supplied over 2500 aristocratic families throughout Europe with dinner services carrying personal crests and monograms, and has a collection of 50,000 manufacturing moulds. Nowadays production uses modern techniques, although traditional methods such as hand painting are still used for some products.

Go ahead over roundabout (Quai de Sully, D951) and bear R to follow gravel track on flood plain below road. Climb back up to road and immediately fork R beside Rue des Iris (sp Port Gallier) past campsite R. Continue out of town under railway viaduct and follow riverside road through hamlet of **Port Gallier**.

Where road ends, continue up cobbled ramp and ahead on gravel track along flood dyke. After 2.5km, pass Les Bordelets farm and bear L off flood dyke on road winding between fields to reach **St Gondon** (19.5km, 131m) (accommodation, refreshments).

Route through village is complicated. Turn sharply R (Rue de l'Ormet) at offset crossroads and fork L at next junction. Cross stream and go ahead through barriers on gravel track over second branch of stream. Cycle up slope and turn L (Rue des Pierres Longues) at next crossroads. Go ahead across main road then bear L (Rue du Parc) to follow road winding through housing development. At end, turn R (Rte de St Florent, D54) and continue, gently undulating through fields and woods, to **St Florent** (25km, 144m) (accommodation, refreshments). ▶

The cooling towers and reactors of Dampierre nuclear power station can be seen on other side of Loire to the right.

At T-junction in village centre turn sharply R (Rue de Sully, D63). Continue out of village into forest and after 750m fork R (sp Lion-en-Sullias). Continue ahead through fields and forest to reach edge of **Lion-en-Sullias** (29.5km, 125m) (accommodation).

Go ahead over two crossroads into Rue du Cimetière, then continue out of village and bear L (Rte du Val) through Bois du Val forest. After 2.5km, bear R then dogleg R and L onto cycle track along flood dyke. Continue parallel with Loire, passing Gorgeats farm L (accommodation), to reach road. Follow this past château parkland

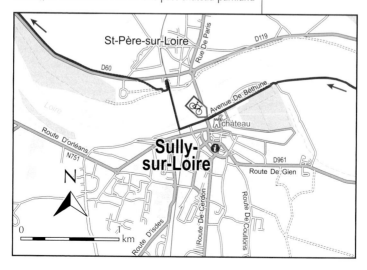

133

Sully-sur-Loire Château is one of the prettiest châteaux on the Loire

L to reach moated Château de Sully and crossroads by Loire bridge in **Sully-sur-Loire** (40.5km, 111m) (accommodation, refreshments, tourist office).

Sully-sur-Loire (pop 5300) is dominated by its picture-postcard pretty château. Built originally as a medieval fortress commanding a crossing point of the Loire, it was redeveloped by Maximilien de Béthune (1560–1641) as a stately home surrounded by a moat with formal gardens and a deer park. It remained in family hands until 1962, since when it has been municipally owned. Inside is a large collection of period furniture, tapestries, paintings and sculpture. Famous visitors include Louis XIV, who took temporary refuge after being driven out of Paris in 1652, and Voltaire, who stayed here between 1716 and 1719 after exile from the capital for lampooning public morals.

STAGE 15
Sully-sur-Loire to Orléans

Start	Sully-sur-Loire, château (111m)
Finish	Orléans, George V bridge (99m)
Distance	50.5km
Waymarking	Loire à Vélo

Initially crossing to the north of the Loire, then crossing back to the south bank before halfway, this completely flat stage mostly follows flood dykes with a few short stretches on quiet roads. There are two main sights just off-route. Both are religious buildings: a great Benedictine monastery at St Benoît-sur-Loire and one of France's oldest churches at Germigny-des-Prés.

From outside château in **Sully-sur-Loire**, follow road (Ch de la Levée) W beside Loire. Turn R across river on cycle track using renovated railway bridge. On opposite bank, bear L back towards river then circle car park behind bollards R. Turn R and fork R past allotments to reach and cross main road (Rue d'Orléans, D60).

Descend to cross side road and follow cycle track parallel with road running below flood dyke. After 3km turn L across main road and continue on cycle track along flood dyke beside river, passing hamlets of Les Places (4.5km, 112m) (accommodation), **Les Prouteaux** and Les Braudins.

Where asphalt ends, turn L off flood dyke on gravel track winding through woods. Emerge onto road by entrance to campsite L and turn R. After 75m, fork R to follow one-way circulation through settlement of Le Port. Continue past fork R that leads to **St Benoît-sur-Loire** (8km, 111m) (accommodation, refreshments, camping, tourist office).

After passing turn-off, follow flood dyke and just before reaching main road (D60) drop down R off dyke.

ST BENOÎT-SUR-LOIRE

King Philippe I is buried in St Benoît abbey

St Benoît-sur-Loire (pop 2000) is the site of Fleury Abbey, a Benedictine monastery that is one of the oldest in France. Founded in AD651, it holds the remains of the order's founder St Benedict, which were moved here from Monte Cassino (Italy). The original abbey was destroyed by the Normans in 1026; in its place was raised a great Romanesque-style basilica built between 1027 and 1218. By 1108 the building was sufficiently complete to allow burial of King Philippe I, who, as a devotee of St Benedict, had asked to be buried here rather than in the royal mausoleum at St Denis. The abbey was suppressed during the Revolution and was not reoccupied until 1864. The present-day community numbers about 40 brothers, who live by the sale of craft items (particularly sweets in the shape of monks) and from the revenue generated by 100,000 visitors and pilgrims annually.

The gatehouse and Gauzlin tower, part of which predates the 1026 destruction, is the iconic symbol of the abbey with 12 enormous columns sculpted with biblical episodes and scenes of rural life. Outside the church the north portal, which was the entrance for local villagers, is richly decorated, while inside the church King Philippe's tomb is in the choir and St Benedict's remains are in the crypt.

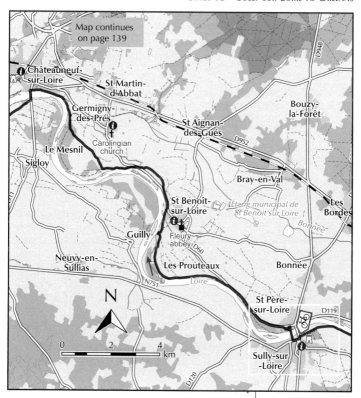

Cross road and continue on cycle track below flood dyke, passing sewerage works R. After 600m emerge on side road and bear R, winding through Les Boutrons hamlet (11.5km, 108m).

Pass equestrian centre R and bear R below dyke parallel with road (D60). After 200m, turn L and cross road to follow gravel track along flood dyke beside river. After 1.4km turn R off dyke onto quiet road (Ch des Marois) and fork L through agricultural hamlet of Les Marois. Fork L again (Rte du Mesnil) and continue through **Le Mesnil** (15.5km, 107m).

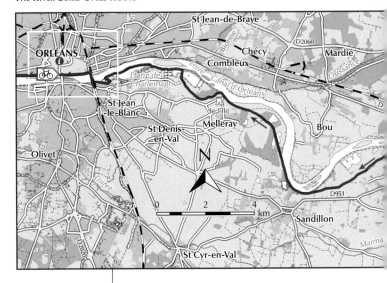

In the village of **Germigny-des-Prés** (1.5km north-east of Le Mesnil) is a Carolingian church built in AD806 which claims to be the oldest in France. Built in the shape of a Greek cross with a cupola, the highlight is a 130,000-piece mosaic that decorates the apse.

Fork L in middle of hamlet (Ch de la Plage) and continue through woods. Where road ends cycle ahead on gravel track. Bear L on bridge over Bonnée stream and continue on Loire riverbank. Cross bridge over side-stream and bear L. Where track ahead narrows, fork R to reach road and bear L. After 50m, fork L back to riverbank and continue ahead. Where track forks, R fork winding through woods is official cycle route (riverside promenade is pedestrians only) but this can get very muddy when wet. Emerge onto road (Quai Penthièvre) and continue to **Châteauneuf** bridge (19km, 107m) (accommodation, refreshments, camping, tourist office, cycle shop).

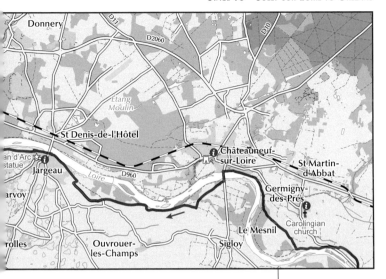

Châteauneuf-sur-Loire (pop 8200) gets its name from an 11th-century fort built to control a crossing point of the Loire. This was redeveloped in the 17th century as a château for French statesman Louis Phélypeaux (1598–1681), with a landscaped park and arboretum. Most of the building has been demolished and what remains houses the town hall. Phélypeaux is buried in a baroque tomb in the nearby church.

Turn L over Loire (Rte de Châteauneuf, D10). At bridge end, turn R (sp Les Vallées) on asphalt road to reach Les Vallées (21km, 104m). Turn R on cycle track along flood dyke and continue for 4km. Just before La Bourdonnière hamlet, drop down L onto road (D107) and continue through La Fontaine-St Vrain and Les Sablons hamlets.

Where road reaches flood dyke, turn R on road below dyke then ascend cobbled ramp and turn L along dyke. Emerge onto road (Rue du 71ème BCP), and opposite

The ramp is easy to miss.

road junction, just before first house on riverbank, drop steeply down R on cobbled ramp towards river. ◄ Bear R on gravel track along riverbank and pass under Loire bridge in **Jargeau** (28.5km, 103m) (accommodation, refreshments, camping, tourist office).

> **Jargeau** (pop 4600) was a medieval walled town surrounding an old abbey. The walls have long gone, but their route can be traced by the wide boulevards that ring the town centre. In the battle of Jargeau (1429) Jeanne d'Arc was wounded but still helped the French capture the town from the English. A plaque commemorating her role in the battle is on the Porte Madeleine old city gate and her statue is in Pl Martroy. As a reward for their role in helping Jeanne d'Arc in the battle, local butchers were given the right to produce a special sausage – the *andouille-Jargeau*, made from 60 per cent pork meat and 40 per cent offal. Since 1971 the 'Brotherhood of the Knights of the Tasty Sausage' have organised a festival and annual competition to find the best andouille.

Viewpoint R overlooking the Loire is on the abutment of an old suspension bridge, dismantled when the current bridge opened in 1988.

Continue ahead beside river and emerge onto road. ◄ Follow road to reach entrance to campsite. Turn sharply L, climb away from river and turn R then fork R along flood dyke. Pass turn-off to **Sandillon** (35.5km, 95m) (accommodation, refreshments) and large aggregate workings (both L), continuing along flood dyke. Pass extensive market gardens on sandy soil at **Melleray** L, and ruins of 16th-century **Château de l'Ile** L (41km, 96m).

At vehicle barrier, fork R, dropping down off flood dyke. Pass car parking area L and continue on concrete track between two former aggregate lakes. Bear L, parallel with Loire, and follow track winding through open woodland. Where track divides, fork R (L track is for pedestrians).

Pass over small bridge, then where tracks recombine, turn R and continue through riparian woodland between lake L and river R. Bear R over another bridge and fork

R to continue alongside **Étang Charlemagne** recreational lake L. Bear R, passing grassy area L, then follow asphalt track as it bears R beside Loire and eventually L away from river.

Turn R over small bridge and R again on track up onto flood dyke. Turn R along dyke and continue to reach embankment of railway bridge over Loire. Turn L beside embankment and continue ahead on road (Rue de l'Ile de Corse). Turn R under railway (cycle track R), then bear R on ramp up to main road and follow cycle track R over Loire road bridge into Orléans.

At end of bridge take ramp R, dropping down and bearing L to reach road. Turn L under ramp, then cross riverside boulevard and turn R on cycle track between boulevard (Quai du Fort Alleaume) and canal, passing lock L. Continue along riverside to reach Pont George V bridge near centre of **Orléans** (50.5km, 99m) (accommodation, refreshments, YH, camping, tourist office, cycle shop, station).

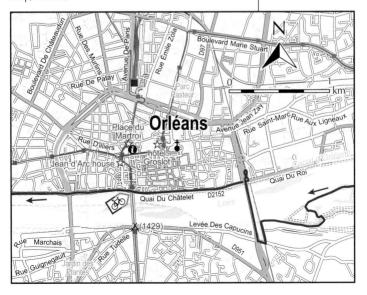

ORLÉANS

The position of Orléans (urban pop 283,000) as the nearest place on the Loire to Paris (approximately 110km) has given it strategic importance over many centuries. A Gallic stronghold, it was captured and Romanised by Julius Caesar (52BC) and later rebuilt by Roman Emperor Aurelian (AD274), who gave his name to the city as Aureliana, which became Orléans. By the Middle Ages it was the seat of the Dukes of Valois-Orléans, a family closely related to the French monarchy. In 1498, Louis of Orléans became king as Louis XII, and from then on the dukedom became a courtesy title given to the king's oldest brother.

Jean d'Arc led French forces to victory at the battle of Orléans (1429)

The city had one of the first bridges over the river, and on the south bank the châtelet des Tourelles guarded the bridge. This was the site of the battle of Orléans (1429), when French forces led by Jeanne d'Arc succeeded in lifting an English siege of the city during the Hundred Years' War. The title 'Maid of Orléans' was conferred upon her and she was given a house in the city that nowadays hosts a museum dedicated to her life. Other memorials to Jeanne include an equestrian statue in Pl du Martroi and stained-glass windows in the cathedral. After the war, Orléans prospered as trade grew between northern France and the south, with merchants paying duties on the goods they transported and tolls to use the bridge. The city became fashionable as successive kings frequently stayed in the city while travelling between Paris and various royal demesnes in the Loire Valley. A number of Renaissance buildings reflect the wealth of this period, including the Hôtel de la Vieille Intendance, formerly the residence of the king when passing through and now used by the administrative court. The Hôtel Groslot, now the town hall, was another stopping-over point for French kings.

Orléans cathedral is lit by a son et lumière display on summer evenings

STAGE 16
Orléans to Beaugency

Start	Orléans, George V bridge (99m)
Finish	Beaugency bridge (89m)
Distance	28km
Waymarking	Loire à Vélo

After Orléans, the Loire turns west between the forests of the Sologne to the south and the fertile Beauce to the north. This short, flat stage starts north of the river and crosses to the south bank before re-crossing at Meung-sur-Loire to end in the small fortified town of Beaugency. Going is on quiet roads, flood dykes and surfaced field tracks.

The Pont de l'Europe bridge near Orléans

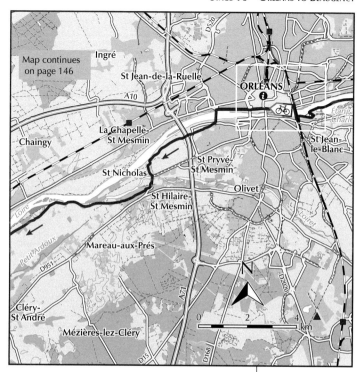

From N end of Pont George V bridge in **Orléans**, follow Quai Cypierre (D2152) W beside Loire on cycle
track L of road. Continue beside Quai Barentin and bear
L to pass under next bridge. Continue beside Quai St
Laurent becoming Quai Madeleine, past fountains of Pl
de l'Europe R, to reach modern Pont de l'Europe bridge.
Turn L over bridge on cycle track R.

At end of bridge continue ahead over main road
then turn R and bear immediately L on quiet road
along flood dyke (Rue des Haute Levées). Just before
roundabout bear R, following cycle track across main
road, then continue along flood dyke on opposite side
of roundabout. Pass under motorway, following flood

dyke for 2km. Pass stone cross L and after 250m turn L off dyke through barriers onto road (Rue Claude Joliot) winding into **St Nicolas**.

Turn R at T-junction (D951) and cross flower-bedecked bridge over Loiret. Join cycle track R of road, and at beginning of **St Hilaire-St Mesmin** (7.5km, 100m)

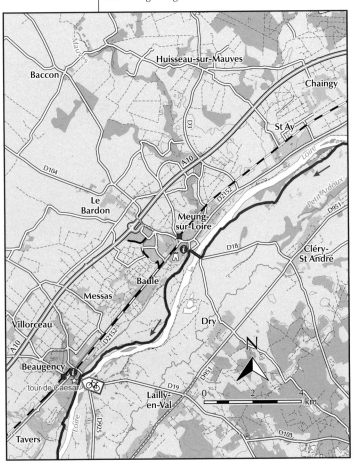

(accommodation, refreshments) follow cycle track R and L away from road around car park. Climb steeply up small alleyway (Venelle de Mauvais Payeurs) and at top turn R again around second car park and continue winding through park. ▸

Emerge onto road (Allée de la Pie) past houses and follow this, bearing L to reach T-junction. Turn R (Rue de Verdun) and continue through village, passing cemetery R. At roundabout fork R (first exit) to follow Rue de Verdun out of village and continue along flood dyke between fields for 6.5km.

Bear R off flood dyke, opposite turning into La Verdaille, onto winding track through fields and woods. Continue beside Loire R, passing Meung weir. Emerge onto quiet road and continue to crossroads. Turn R (D18) to cross Loire on suspension bridge. ▸ Continue on Rue du Pont and turn L onto gravel track through avenue of trees with car park R in **Meung-sur-Loire** (20km, 90m) (accommodation, refreshments, tourist office, station).

The half-timbered building on the right is the former Château de la Pie, now the town hall.

The road over the bridge is narrow with no cycle lane.

MEUNG-SUR-LOIRE

Meung-sur-Loire (pop 6500) was the site of a Gallo-Roman village that was destroyed by invading Alans in AD408. Legend has it that the battlefield was cleaned up by St Liphard who channelled three rivers through the site, their waters becoming mauve with blood, giving the name to the river flowing through the village. He built a chapel by the river, which would be developed into a monastery and would eventually hold his remains. The 11th-century church, built to a clover-leaf design with three apses, still houses the relics.

The nearby château, which was built as a country residence for the bishops of Orléans, has dungeons displaying items of medieval torture. By the 19th century the steadily flowing river Mauves had become a location for 38 mills producing flour, paper and dyestuffs. Although 29 can still be identified, none are operating.

Meung has an unusual 20th-century literary connection: *Inspector Maigret*, a Parisian detective in novels by Georges Simenon, takes his holidays in Meung and retires to the town when his crime-solving days are over. One novel, *Ceux de Grande Café*, is entirely set here and there are over 50 references in Simenon's other novels.

Beaugency's medieval bridge has 23 arches

Emerge on road and go ahead L past sports club L. Where road ends continue ahead on gravel track through trees. At T-junction turn R over Mauves and L to continue on gravel track along flood dyke. Continue beside Mauves to reach Loire riverbank and follow track between fields R and riparian forest L.

Pass two small lakes R and turn L at T-junction. Continue on quiet road to reach beginning of Beaugency. Cross small bridge and continue on cobbled track through car park. Turn R in car park then L through avenue of trees beside main road R to reach crossroads beside Loire bridge in **Beaugency** (28km, 89m) (accommodation, refreshments, camping, tourist office, cycle shop, station).

Beaugency (pop 7500) was a medieval fortified town that became part of France in 1292. Part of the walls, including towers and old gatehouses, are still standing. The most notable old building is the 11th-century Tour de Caesar, a 36m-high defensive tower wrongly attributed to the Romans that was incorporated into the castle in the 16th century. The 12th-century Loire bridge has 23 arches and originally had a pilgrim's chapel partway across. The monastic buildings of the former Notre-Dame abbey have been converted into a luxury hotel, while the St Firmin bell tower is all that remains of an 11th-century church that was demolished during the Revolution. Its carillon plays a stanza from a tune dating back to the Hundred Years' War.

STAGE 17
Beaugency to Blois

Start	Beaugency bridge (89m)
Finish	Blois, Jacques Gabriel bridge (72m)
Distance	34.5km (45.5km via Chambord)
Waymarking	Loire à Vélo

The Loire truly becomes the 'Royal River' in this stage with châteaux appearing thick and fast, encompassing every size from great royal summer residences to comfortable country homes for minor nobility. The direct route stays on the north bank, going straight to Blois where there is a former royal château. An alternative route crosses the river to visit the spectacular Château de Chambord, surrounded by its own deer forest, before going on to Blois. This generally flat stage mostly follows flood dykes, quiet country roads and field paths.

From Loire bridge in **Beaugency**, follow quayside south (Quai de l'Abbaye) then keep L (Promenade de Barchelin) past section of old town walls, staying beside river. Where road ends continue ahead on gravel track into open country. Pass below Barchelin and just after sewerage works L, turn L towards river. Turn R on cycle track parallel with river, passing **Tavers** (accommodation, refreshments). Continue ahead for 5km, then follow track bearing R away from river into **Lestiou** (7.5km, 84m).

Turn L onto narrow road (Rue Basse) and continue through edge of village to reach main road (Rue André Spire). Bear L on cycle track L of road, and where road bears R keep ahead on cycle track, following Loire. With St Laurent-des-Eaux **nuclear power station** on opposite bank, zigzag R and L onto flood dyke and continue alongside Loire. ◄ Where road from R joins flood dyke, follow dyke, curving R and L, then continue through forest and farmland for 6km to reach crossroads.

R turn just before the zigzag leads to Avaray (refreshments).

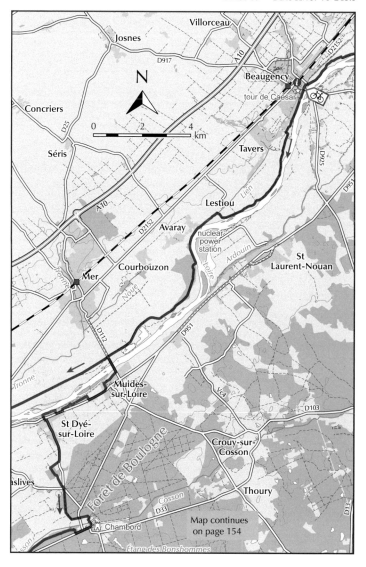

Map continues
on page 154

151

Between Muides-sur-Loire bridge and Blois there is a choice of routes. The main waymarked route continues along the R bank of the Loire for 19km directly to Blois. An alternative crosses the river to visit Chambord, the most spectacular of all the Loire châteaux, before continuing on the L bank to re-join the main route opposite Blois.

Chambord alternative

Turn L across Loire bridge (D112, sp Muides-sur-Loire) on cycle lane R, then R at crossroads (Ave de la Loire) into **Muides-sur-Loire** (17km, 80m) (refreshments, camping).

Continue along flood dyke, passing campsite R, then bear L uphill (Rue de la Créssonnière). Follow road, turning L into Rue de l'Église then R at crossroads (Rue du Tramway). Turn R at T-junction onto main road (D951) with cycle track R. Where cycle track ends, turn R (sp Colliers) and L (Rue des Chênes) to reach T-junction. Turn R (Rue des Piécerots) and follow road, bearing L then L again (Rue du 8 Mai), returning to main road. Turn R on cycle track R of road into beginning of St Dyé-sur-Loire. Turn R (Rue de Bel-Air) and L beside Loire (Quai de Loire). After 500m, turn L away from river (Rue de l'Église), passing church L to reach centre of **St Dyé-sur-Loire** (21km, 88m) (accommodation, refreshments).

Dog-leg L and R over main road into narrow Rue Beaugency. Turn L at T-junction (Rue du Flanc) and R at end into Rte de Chambord. Follow road forking R and at end of village continue on cycle track R of road. Follow cycle track, bearing R away from road into beginning of **Forêt de Boulogne**.

Turn L at junction of tracks and continue winding through forest to regain road. Turn R and after 50m bear L through gates of deer park with château visible ahead. Fork immediately R through barriers onto track through forest and continue, bearing L between forest L and fields R.

Where forest ends, ignore cycle route, which continues ahead across open field. Instead fork L then turn L on unmade track alongside forest L. Dog-leg R and L across road then fork L past seasonal car parks R. At next road, turn R towards château then fork R and continue over canalised river Cosson to reach visitor centre of **Château de Chambord** R (27km, 79m) (refreshments).

CHÂTEAU DE CHAMBORD

Château de Chambord was built as an extravagant hunting lodge for King François I

The central part of the most spectacular Loire château, Château de Chambord, was built between 1519 and 1537 to the orders of François I on the site of an old hunting lodge in the Forêt de Boulogne. Designed by Italian architects (Leonardo da Vinci contributed the central staircase), its construction employed 1800 men. Later kings Henri II and Louis XIV made additions, and when completed in 1685 it had 440 rooms, 365 chimneys and 84 staircases. Outside, the river Cosson was diverted to form a moat around the château and a 32km wall, the longest in France, was built around the game park. Despite its huge size, Chambord was principally a hunting lodge enjoyed by a series of kings until 1725 when it was given by Louis XV to his father-in-law, the exiled king of Poland. By 1789 it had fallen into neglect and its interiors and furnishings were stripped during the Revolution. It reverted briefly to use as a royal residence in the 1820s before falling once again into neglect. It was bought by the state in 1930 with restoration beginning in the 1970s, and the rooms now contain thousands of objects (furniture, paintings and tapestries), although few have historic links with the original building.

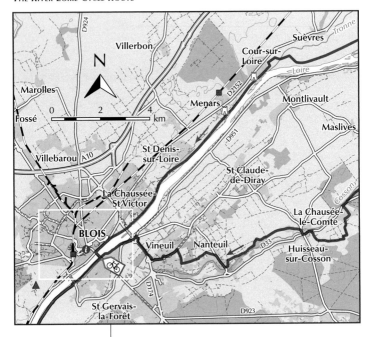

Continue past visitor centre and turn R at triangular junction following cycle track beside Rte Charles X, D33. Pass turn-off R for château parking (D112) and turn R (sp Pont des Italiens) on gravel track into forest. Turn L on cycle track through forest and continue for 2.5km to emerge on main road. Turn R (D33) and pass through exit gates of deer park into **La Chaussée le Comte** (30.5km, 80m) (accommodation, refreshments, camping).

Turn immediately L at crossroads (Rue de Bracieux) then turn R at offset crossroads (still Rue de Bracieux). Turn L (Ch des Perrières) and continue ahead, winding through vineyards for 2km to reach Rue de Châtillon at beginning of next village. Pass cemetery L then turn R at first T-junction and L at second onto main road (Rte de Chambord, D33). Turn L, passing church R, into **Huisseau-sur-Cosson** (34km, 79m) (refreshments, camping).

Turn R (Rue du Pont, D72), then cross river Cosson using cyclist bridge L and fork L (Rue de Biou). Fork L at floral roundabout (second exit, Rue de l'Oisilière) and continue winding through fields and vineyards. Fork R and pass under old railway bridge. Continue through fields then turn L at five-way junction of tracks (Rue du Parc) and continue to reach T-junction. Turn R (Rue de Nanteuil) into **Nanteuil** (38.5km, 83m).

Fork R at roundabout (Ch des Bordes, sp Les Noëls) and after 200m, fork L (Rue des Mangottes). ▶ At village end, turn L onto cycle track winding through fields. Emerge onto road beside cemetery (Ch de la Boisgerbeuse, cycle track R) and continue ahead to reach road. Turn R (Rue du Stade, cycle track R) and pass stadium R. Turn L at T-junction onto main road (Ave des Tailles, cycle track R) and continue past complicated crossroads in **Vineuil** (42km, 83m) (accommodation, refreshments).

Go ahead beside Ave Paul Valéry then follow cycle track bearing R (Rue André Chénier) and turn L across road onto cycle track circling behind housing development (Pl Jules Verne). Turn R (Ave Général de Gaulle, cycle track R), cross side road and turn R at roundabout (Rue des Quatre Vents, first exit) on cycle lane L. Fork L, still Rue des Quatre Vents, and continue ahead on cycle track beside motorway to reach roundabout. Cross first road, then bear L over second exit and L again to follow cycle track beside third exit (D951). Pass under motorway and continue ahead past second roundabout. Bear R away from road, then L beside Loire.

After 600m, dog-leg L and R onto quiet road between main road L and river R. Fork R to continue below main road, then follow cycle track up second ramp L to emerge beside Quai Henri Chavigny. Continue beside Quai Amédée Constant to re-join main route at S end of bridge over Loire, opposite **Blois** (45.5km, 72m).

Main route

Continue ahead on road along flood dyke for another 7km. Cross river Tronne and turn L at T-junction into La

Rue des Mangottes is no entry with permitted use by cyclists.

BLOIS

Henri IV's bedroom in the Château de Blois

The centre of Blois (pop 46,000) is dominated by the Royal Château de Blois. The residence of several French kings, it consists of four wings constructed between the 13th and 17th centuries around a central courtyard. There are 564 rooms, of which 100 are bedrooms, and 75 staircases. The oldest part is the 13th-century Gothic Salle des États Généraux, so named because it housed meetings of the States-General, an early form of French parliament that advised the monarch. King Louis XII (1462–1515) was born here and during his reign Blois became the political capital of France. François I added a wing in Italian Renaissance style, including an external spiral staircase that is the most renowned feature of the building. Henri III (1551–1589) ruled from Blois after being driven out of Paris during the Wars of Religion, and after his assassination Henri IV, the first Bourbon king of France, continued the royal inhabitancy of the château. In 1626 Louis XIII gave the building to his brother and its connection with royalty came to an end. It was abandoned in 1660 and by the time of the Revolution (1789) was in a state of disrepair. The contents, particularly royal statues and coats of arms, were removed and the immense building was turned into a barracks. Restoration started in 1841 and it became a museum. Nowadays the château is owned by the local municipality and is a major tourist attraction with a spectacular son et lumière show on summer evenings.

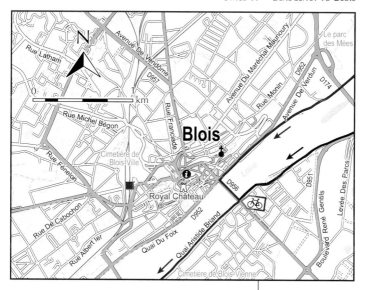

Nuzée hamlet. Fork L in village and continue to **Cour-sur-Loire** (23.5km, 85m). Go ahead over staggered cross-roads (Rue de la Mairie) then turn L at second crossroads (Rue de la Loire). Pass through Pl de la Fontaine then follow road bearing R (Quai de la Loire) beside Tronne. Pass confluence of Tronne with Loire L and small château R. Where riverside road ends, continue ahead through barriers on gravel cycle track, passing **Château de Menars** R (26km, 74m).

Originally built in 1642, **Château de Menars** was bought in 1760 by Mme de Pompadour, official mistress of Louis XV, who greatly extended the building. The château is surrounded by extensive gardens with follies and statuary. A 4km avenue of lime trees is the longest in Europe.

After the Revolution, the château became a college. In the 20th century, Menars was owned by French glass-making company St Gobain who used it as an executive conference and training centre. Put up for sale when the company was nationalised in 1982, it was bought by Lebanese-born property developer Edmond Baysari for £2 million. Over a period of 30 years Baysari spent £100 million restoring the property where he hosted a summit between Ronald Reagan and Mikhail Gorbachev, and entertained such diverse guests as Mick Jagger and the Prince of Wales. Since he died intestate in 2018 the property has been put up for sale with a €30 million asking price. It is likely to become an international hotel although Russian oligarchs and Middle Eastern oil sheiks have shown interest.

Fork R after château then continue along flood dyke for 6km. Pass under disued railway bridge, then emerge on road and follow this under motorway to reach bridge in **Blois** (34.5km, 72m) (accommodation, refreshments, YH, tourist office, station). Turn L over bridge to reach end of stage and to continue directly onto Stage 18.

STAGE 18

Blois to Amboise

Start	Blois, Jacques Gabriel bridge (72m)
Finish	Amboise, Quai Général de Gaulle (59m)
Distance	42km
Waymarking	Loire à Vélo

The Royal River continues past more great châteaux at Chaumont and Amboise. This stage, which is mostly on quiet roads south of the Loire, partly follows flat land beside the river but makes three short 30–50m climbs onto the chalk plateau bordering the river valley.

From S end of Pont Jacques Gabriel bridge opposite **Blois**, drop down W on cobbled ramp to reach cycle track beside river. Continue under next bridge and turn sharply L to reach roundabout. Turn R then cross first exit road and continue on cycle track below flood dyke L of road (Ch de la Rabière) for 3km. Follow track as it bears L away from road and zigzags around small industrial area. At T-junction, cross road and turn R on cycle track beside road (D91) then follow this bearing L at next junction beside D751. Cycle track switches to R and continues over river Cosson to reach beginning of **Chailles** (6.5km, 68m) (refreshments).

Turn R through park and bear L alongside Cosson. Continue winding through parkland then curve L to reach T-junction. Turn R (Rue de la Vallée) then follow road bearing L and turn R into woodland. Pass sewerage works R and go ahead at crossroads. Continue ahead to reach high stone wall L then turn L (Rue de la Fontaine), beside wall R. ▶ Turn R at triangular junction (Rue de la Loire) into old village of **Madon** (11km, 85m).

There has been a castle on the site of **Château Madon** since medieval times. Originally a

The stone wall surrounds the park of Château Madon, the entrance to which is passed on the right.

military structure to defend against attacks upriver by Vikings and Normans, it was sacked by the English during the Hundred Years' War. Rebuilt from 1468, it became first a Benedictine monastery (where Louis XII came in 1498 to seek annulment of his marriage) and after 1698 a summer palace for the bishops of Blois. Rebuilt again (1770) in its current form by Bishop Termont, it was confiscated only a few years later when ecclesiastical properties were seized during the Revolution.

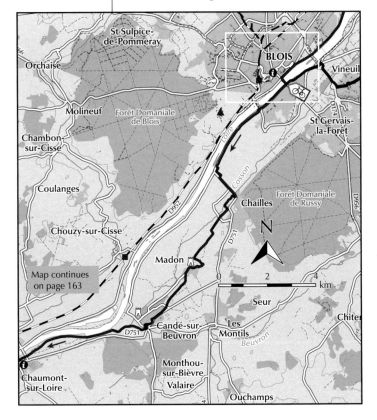

Map continues on page 163

Pass bus shelter R and turn R, keeping beside wall of park (still Rue de la Loire), to continue through village. At end of Madon, fork L (Rue de l'Aumône) into l'Aumône hamlet. Fork L uphill (Rue des Châtaigniers) and where road ends continue ahead on sandy track. Go ahead over crossroads and emerge beside main road. Continue on cycle track R, eventually bearing R away from road past small shopping area R. Turn L (Rue des Ficaudières) at crossroads and follow this, curving R downhill. Turn R (Rue de l'Église) and bear L downhill past church L. Turn L at T-junction (Rue du Château, D173) to reach centre of **Candé-sur-Beuvron** (14.5km, 68m) (accommodation, refreshments, camping).

The old bridge at Candé-sur-Beuvron is reserved for cyclists

> The hillside village of **Candé-sur-Beuvron** (pop 1500) developed beside a bridge over the Beuvron just above its confluence with the Loire. The small château is now a seminary for the community of St Martin.

At beginning of village square, turn R over cycle bridge (the old bridge) – turning is easy to miss – across

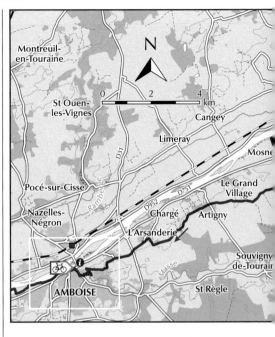

To reach the centre
of Chaumont, turn
L after the bridge.

river Beuvron, and R again on gravel track beside river.
Follow this to reach Loire and continue parallel with river
for 4km. Emerge onto road by campsite R and continue
under road bridge to reach edge of **Chaumont-sur-Loire**
(20.5km, 63m) (accommodation, refreshments, camping,
tourist office). ◀

Continue ahead with riverside meadows R and village L and pass below **Château de Chaumont** on ridge
rising steeply behind village. Drop down cobbled ramp
and continue on cycle track between road (D751) and
Loire for 2km.

Follow cycle track, turning L across road and forking L on side road winding through trees and climbing
onto ridge. At top of hill fork R through vineyards to reach
T-junction. Turn L then after 80m turn R at next T-junction
through Le Meunet hamlet. Continue ahead (Rue des

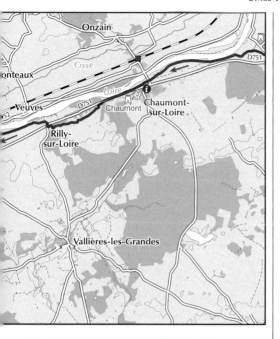

CHAUMONT-SUR-LOIRE

Chaumont-sur-Loire (pop 1100) is dominated by its attractive château. Originally a defensive castle, it was burnt (1465) on the order of Louis XI after the owner (Charles I of Amboise) had supported a rebellion. Reconstructed (1469–1510) by two generations of the family, it became a partly fortified Renaissance-style stately home. After the Chaumont branch of the House of Amboise died out (1525), the château became owned by Catherine de Medici, a Florentine princess who, married French King Henri II and became queen of France. After Henri's death, the château was given to his mistress, Diane de Poitiers and then passed through many hands before being inherited by the wife of Prince Amédée de Broglie (1875). Over 40 years the Broglie family transformed the château and its park into a sumptuous residence. It was one of the first houses in Europe to be fitted with electric lighting, while the stables for the prince's stud of horses were considered

163

Château de Chaumont hosts an annual garden festival

the most luxurious in Europe. Parties and receptions attracted leading members of society until 1938 when financial problems forced the princess to sell the house to the French state.

Now restored as a historic monument, the château and stables attract many visitors. The star attraction, however, is the park, which has hosted an international gardening festival since 1992. Every year 20 designers who have won garden festivals throughout the world are invited to create new gardens in the park on a different annual theme. Open from late April to mid October, the festival attracts about 350,000 visitors annually.

Beaudries) to reach T-junction and turn R (Rue de l'Église) under footbridge, winding downhill into **Rilly-sur-Loire** (25km, 65m) (accommodation).

Turn R at T-junction and immediately bear R onto main road (Rue Nationale, D751) then after 50m fork L (Rue de la Plage) and bear L out of village. Follow track to riverbank and continue through riparian woodland. Emerge onto road and pass campsite L. After 300m follow track bearing L between fields to reach T-junction. Turn L then turn R through woods over small bridge to emerge on road. Continue ahead past village wash-house

L into centre of **Mosnes** (29.5km, 67m) (accommodation, refreshments, camping).

Turn first R opposite church (Rue du Général de Gaulle, D751) and after 60m turn L (Rue des Thomeaux) in front of spa hotel. Bear R (Ch de la Garenne) and climb steeply out of village to reach plateau. ▶ At top of hill, pass large calvary cross L and continue on road through vineyards, then turn R at T-junction (Rte des Montils) through fields across plateau. Pass La Maillardière hamlet and continue through **Le Grand Village** (31.5km, 109m) (accommodation).

The road out of the village is one-way downhill with a contra-flow uphill lane for cyclists.

Go ahead over crossroads then pass water tower L before continuing across plateau past Le Vau hamlet and through **Artigny** (34.5km, 105m) (accommodation) on Rue de la Résistance. Pass water tower R and after 400m fork L (sp St Règle) through vineyards. Go ahead over crossroads (Rue des Têtes Noires) and turn R (Rue des Blaisis) opposite next water tower into **L'Arsanderie** (37.5km, 97m).

Turn L in village (Rue du Clos du Saule) and turn L (Rue de la République) out of village. Continue into Rue des Fauchelleries and cross road bridge over Amboise bypass. Road becomes Rue des Chaumières as it enters Amboise. Where road turns R, keep ahead (Rue de Bel-Air) and follow this, bearing L.

Turn R (Rue Augustin Thierry) through houses then open fields before starting to descend between topiary hedges. Where road bears R towards upper gateway of Château d'Amboise, with view of fortifications ahead, turn sharply L, descending through barrier onto Rue Léonard Perrault.

At bottom of hill, by rear entrance to **Château de Clos Lucé**, turn sharply R (Rue Victor Hugo). ▶ Continue downhill, turning sharply L (Impasse du Moulin), and after 25m turn R on cycle track (Rue de la Vignole) beside car park. Turn R at end of car park along cycle track and turn L to cross serpentine bridge over river Masse.

Rue Victor Hugo is one-way uphill with a contra-flow cycle lane downhill.

Bear L in next car park then follow road bearing R and turn L out of car park. Turn R through yet another car park to reach Pl Richelieu. Leave by turning R (Rue

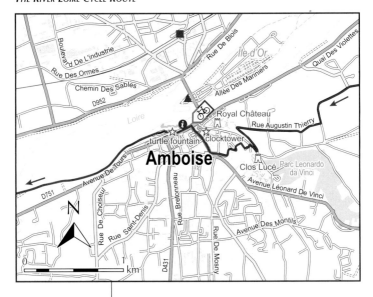

Joyeuse) just before half-timbered Hôtel Le Blason. Continue on Rue d'Orange and ahead into Rue Jean-Jacques Rousseau to reach end of stage at dual carriage-way Quai Général de Gaulle in **Amboise** (42km, 59m) (accommodation, refreshments, camping, tourist office, cycle shop, station).

AMBOISE

The market town of Amboise (pop 12,700) was for 150 years home to the French royal court. The castle, which was built before the 11th century, became a possession of the French crown in 1434. It soon became a royal residence, initially as a place of safety for sons and daughters of the monarch away from the dangers and intrigues of Paris. King Charles VIII (reigned 1483–1498) was born in the castle and when he assumed the throne, he made it his principal royal residence. A passionate fan of Italian culture, he had the Gothic castle transformed into a Renaissance palace. His successor, Louis XII, continued to develop the palace.

The surrealist fountain in Amboise with a teddy bear above a turtle was designed by Max Ernst

During the reign of François I (1515–1547), the Italian artist and inventor Leonardo da Vinci was invited to stay at Amboise and was accommodated in nearby Clos Lucé. He brought with him from Italy three paintings, including the *Mona Lisa*. While in Amboise he continued his inventions, making plans to improve water supply to the palace, drain nearby marshes and design a double helix staircase for the royal palace at Chambord. He died in 1519, allegedly with François by his deathbed, and was buried in the Chapelle St Hubert. Some of his inventions are on display in Clos Lucé.

Henri II continued expanding the palace by adding a new eastern wing, but after Henri III died in 1589 the royal connection ended and in the 17th century the château became a prison for VIP prisoners. Confiscated by the state during the Revolution, two thirds of the palace was demolished under orders of Napoleon. After the restoration of the monarchy, King Louis Philippe restored part of the castle only for it to be confiscated again in 1848. It then became a retirement home before being restored as a tourist attraction in the early 20th century.

The building is regarded as a prime example of Gothic-Renaissance transformational style. Inside, the most important room is the huge Gothic council chamber, where the king met his advisors. Other sights include the Tour d'Horloge clock tower and a surrealist fountain by Max Ernst of a turtle supporting a teddy bear. The narrow streets of the medieval old town contain many half-timbered buildings.

STAGE 19
Amboise to Tours

Start	Amboise, Quai Général de Gaulle (59m)
Finish	Tours, cathedral (58m)
Distance	27km
Waymarking	Loire à Vélo

Low, vineyard-covered chalk hills that form the areas of Vouvray (north) and Montlouis (south), both known for producing white wine, bound the sides of the valley. After leaving Amboise beside the river, the route makes a short climb onto the plateau S of the river to wander through the vineyards of Touraine before descending to Montlouis. The Loire is then closely followed into Tours, principal city of the region.

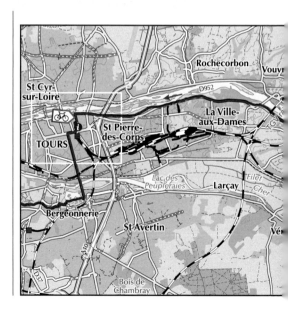

From Quai Général de Gaulle in **Amboise**, cycle W along busy dual carriageway, parallel with Loire. Just before modernist fountain (Fontaine Max Ernst), turn R up and over flood dyke. Continue through car park. Bear R and L to leave car park by NW corner, dropping down on cobbled ramp to river meadow. Climb again to run alongside another car park, behind bollards. Drop down again to follow cycle track parallel with Loire.

Pass aggregates depot L and 1.7km later bear L away from river for 75m, then turn R, passing sewerage works. At next crossing of tracks, turn R to reach river and follow track bearing L between Étang de la Varenne-sous-Chandon lake L and Loire R. At end of lake bear R through trees to reach main road. Turn R (D751) on cycle track R to reach **Lussault-sur-Loire** (5.5km, 59m) (refreshments).

Just before village church, turn L across main road, then pass church and turn L (Rue du Village, D283), climbing steadily. Fork L by metal wayside cross and

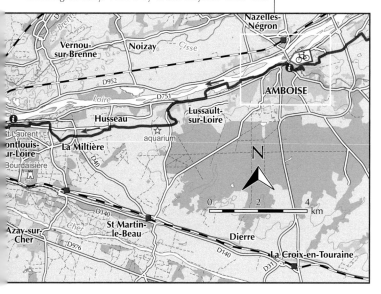

House 25 on the left has an unusual front wall topped by over 200 multicoloured jugs and teapots.

after 50m turn L (Rue Vallée St Martin), still climbing past houses and wine cellars cut into cliff face L. ◀ Turn R at T-junction (Rte des Montils, D283) and go ahead over crossroads out of village on cycle track L.

Pass **Aquarium du Val de Loire**, which sits behind extensive car parks L. Pass road junction R then fork R (sp Montlouis) on cycle track into scrubland. Continue across plateau then bear R on road (Rue des Marronniers) and go ahead through edge of **Husseau** (9.5km, 86m) (accommodation).

At end of village, turn L at crossroads and after 100m turn R on track through vineyards to reach T-junction in **La Miltière** (11.5km, 64m).

Turn L then immediately R before road junction on narrow lane beside house 53. Continue ahead through vineyards and bear half-R at crossing of five tracks. Bear R onto road and continue over crossroads (Rue de Bondésir) past water tower L. Fork L (Rue des Hauts de Loire), keeping along edge of plateau with views over Loire R. Bear R at T-junction (Rue du 4 Août 1789) and after 60m fork L (still Rue du 4 Août 1789).

Continue into Ch Tourne and follow this, turning L to reach T-junction. Turn R (Rue Madeleine Vernet) and continue on Rue du Maréchal Foch into centre of **Montlouis-sur-Loire** (15km, 73m) (accommodation, refreshments, camping, tourist office, station).

Along with the eponymous village of Vouvray on the other side of the river, **Montlouis-sur-Loire** (pop 11,000) is part of the Touraine wine-producing region. Chenin blanc grapes are used to produce relatively light but long-lasting dry and medium-sweet white wines. However, as the weather is a variable, vintages vary from season to season and in poor years some of the harvest is used to produce Crémant de la Loire, a méthode champenoise sparkling wine.

St Laurent church has a modern stained-glass window depicting the bombing of the Loire bridge in 1944. Château de la Bourdaisière (2km S of

town overlooking the Val du Cher) is nowadays
a luxury hotel, although its grounds contain the
French national tomato conservatory with over
500 varieties of tomato.

Bear L beside old water pump (Rue Clémenceau),
and where road opens out into square in front of town
hall, turn R into narrow alleyway (Rue des Grippeaux).
Continue ahead on road and bear R at T-junction (Rue
Descartes, D85). Turn R at crossroads (Rue du Saule
Michaud) and pass under railway bridge. Turn immediately R on cycle track beside railway.

At end, beside station R, turn R using cycle track L
and just before reaching main road turn L on cycle track
parallel with road. Dog-leg L past swimming pools then
bear R and L on track, passing campsite L, and continue
to main road. Cross this road onto slip road opposite,
then turn L and bear R onto cycle track beside Loire.

Continue under railway and road bridges. ▸ Zigzag
L and R over flood dyke, then bear R to join cycle track
along flood dyke. Follow this as it drops down below
dyke and runs beside main road past **La Ville-aux-Dames**.

The railway bridge
carries the TGV-
Aquitaine high-speed
line from Paris to
southwest France.

Continue along cycle track below main road
(D751) for 4.5km, then follow track bearing away from
road beside Loire for 1km before returning to roadside.
Follow cycle track between road and river under motorway bridge and straight ahead across approach to Pont
Mirabeau bridge. Just before St Symphorien suspension
bridge, turn L across main road into Rue Lavoisier past
Tours château L to reach cathedral L in centre of **Tours**
(27km, 58m) (accommodation, refreshments, tourist
office, cycle shop, station).

TOURS

Tours (urban pop 360,000) sits on a peninsula between the rivers Loire and
Cher. It developed as a Roman city (Caesarodunum) with the fifth-largest
amphitheatre in the Roman empire, although little remains. Its transforma-
tion from colonial Roman city to the principal city of the Loire basin is linked

to the life of St Martin (AD316–397), the son of a Roman soldier who went on to become patron saint of France. After serving in the Roman cavalry he developed a Christian faith, eventually becoming bishop of Tours (AD371), where he established a monastery at Marmoutier on the north side of the Loire opposite the city. After he died, his tomb in Tours became a major pilgrim destination and an essential stopover point for pilgrims from northern Europe on their way to Santiago de Compostela. He was adopted by successive royal houses of France as a figure of veneration, probably due to his dual role as soldier and saint. A piece of cloak attributed to an act of charity performed by Martin was preserved and became an important holy relic, venerated by early French kings and their subjects – to the extent that

Napoleon planted a cedar in the grounds of the archbishop's palace in Tours

oaths of allegiance were taken over the cloak and it was carried into battle beside the king by royal chaplains. The tomb and relics continued to draw pilgrims to Tours for many centuries until both the abbey at Marmoutier and the basilica holding the tomb in Tours were pulled down during the Revolution. The Franco-Prussian War (1870–1871) led to a revival of interest in St Martin as a soldier-saint offering protection against the German threat. His tomb was excavated and a small chapel built, in which banners were blessed before being taken into battle. In 1925 a new basilica was consecrated over the tomb. Tours is unusual in having two medieval city centres. The first, a religious and administrative area, grew up around the old Roman castrum, where you can find the cathedral, archbishop's palace and castle. The second, Châteauneuf (nowadays confusingly called Vieux Tours), 1km to the west around the abbey of St Martin and the market, became the medieval economic and commercial centre. Here there are narrow streets with preserved half-timbered buildings, and Pl Plumereau, filled with bars and restaurants. The area between the two became developed from the 14th

Pl Plumerau is the heart of the old town in Tours

century onwards, although much of this was redeveloped in the 20th century using a grid system. At the same time the old city became one of the first conservation areas in France.

The principal building is the magnificent cathedral, built between 1170 and 1547. This long period of construction led to the use of three different styles: Romanesque elements for the lower walls and buttresses, Gothic for most of the building and its ornamentation, and Renaissance for the tops of the towers. The nearby archbishop's palace is now the museum of fine art. Within its grounds there is an ancient cedar planted by Napoleon in 1804 and a stuffed elephant called Fritz that was shot after escaping from Barnum and Bailey's circus in 1902.

The language spoken in Tours is said to be 'perfect French', without any regional accents (an equivalent to Oxford English), regarded as standard pronunciation. A good place to try out your language skills?

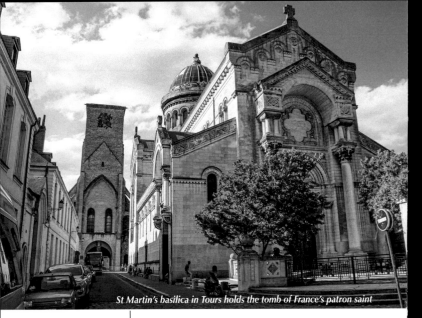
St Martin's basilica in Tours holds the tomb of France's patron saint

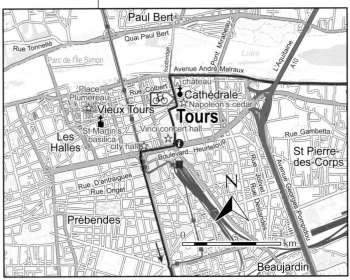

STAGE 20

Tours to Bréhémont

Start	Tours, cathedral (58m)
Finish	Bréhémont, church (38m)
Distance	35km
Waymarking	Loire à Vélo

After an exit from Tours mostly through parkland, the route follows well-surfaced field paths and minor roads alongside the Cher to reach its confluence with the Loire, then continues on a quiet road along flood dykes to the small riverside village of Bréhémont where there is limited accommodation.

From Pl de la Cathédrale in front of **Tours cathedral**, continue S (Rue Lavoisier) into Pl François-Sicard. Turn R around square and leave by turning L in opposite corner (Rue Bernard Palissy). ▶ Pass modern La Vinci congress and concert hall R, and turn R through gardens in middle of dual carriageway Bvd Heurteloup.

Continue to reach road with tram tracks and turn L (Ave du Grammont) to follow cycle lane in service road beside main road. Continue ahead over two roundabouts and two bridges over branches of river Cher (cycle track R). Pass Centre Aquatique du Lac R, then fork R (Rue de l'Auberdière) and turn R beside small roundabout into Parc Bergeonnerie.

Immediately fork L through barrier, passing car park R, onto cycle track winding through park beside lake R. Before end of lake, turn L and immediately L again through barrier to reach T-junction. Turn L over small bridge and R onto cycle track beside main road (Ave Marcel Dassault). Just before next roundabout, turn L across road and follow cycle track beside road, turning L (Rte des Deux Lions).

After 60m turn R onto cycle track (Allée André Besse) and follow this, winding through parkland behind series

Rue Bernard Palissy is a one-way street with contra-flow cycling permitted.

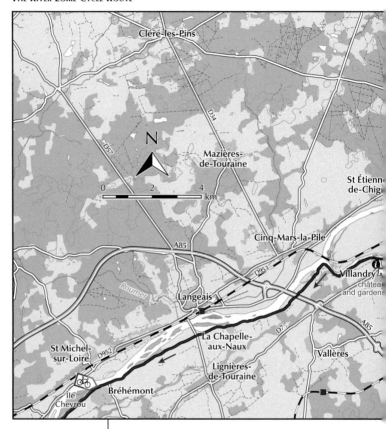

of small factory units in high-tech industrial park R. Bear L at T-junction, continuing to wind through park. Turn L, going under road and tram bridges into open country with town of **Joué-lès-Tours** (7km, 47m) (accommodation, camping) visible on hillside L.

Pass **Château de Beaulieu** L and follow road circling golf course R. Cross main road onto cycle track through fields. Bear R, parallel with motorway, and continue over crossroads to reach river Cher. Turn L under motorway

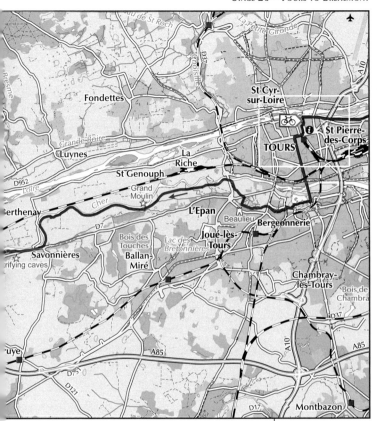

along riverbank. Pass landing stage for Joué R and continue through woods and fields away from the river for 3km to reach **Le Grand Moulin** (12.5km, 45m) (refreshments). ▶

Bear R to pass between mill buildings and continue along riverbank, passing La Grange (16km, 45m) (accommodation). Where road bears L away from river, turn R to continue along riverbank, passing between campsite and river to reach quayside in **Savonnières** (18.5km, 43m) (accommodation, refreshments, camping, station).

Le Grand Moulin is a picturesque mill on an island in the river Cher.

Château de Villandry was the last great renaissance castle built on the Loire

Savonnières (pop 3150) grew up around a small port on the river Cher. Nowadays it is a leading location for the renovation and reconstruction of traditional Loire scutes and a number can be seen moored on the riverbank.

The newer residential part of town sits above the river on top of a limestone hillside. Under this hillside is a warren of natural caves with stalactites, stalagmites and other limestone features. The caves, which are open to visitors and can be entered from the riverside road, are known as the 'petrifying grottoes' due to the ability of the highly calcareous water to turn items to stone.

Continue on riverbank road (Rue des Saules), passing weir R. At square opposite St Gervais church, drop down ahead onto riverbank cycle track. Pass under bridge and below entrance to limestone caves, then continue beside river past road L that leads to **Villandry** (21km, 42m) (accommodation, refreshments, tourist office). ◄

Villandry is 500m L off-route.

Continue on riverside road (D16), and where this turns away from river just after 28km stone, turn R

VILLANDRY

Villandry (pop 1125) has a modest (by Loire standards) château surrounded by one of the most spectacular gardens in France. The château, completed around 1536, was the last great Renaissance castle built on the Loire. It changed hands in 1754 and was remodelled with higher standards of comfort, including more windows, balconies, a new staircase and an English-style garden. However, successive owners allowed the building to fall into disrepair and the gardens to become overgrown. In 1906, when the château was about to be demolished, it was bought by Dr Joachim Carvallo, a Spanish medical scientist, and his wealthy American wife, and they set about restoring the building and filling it with old master paintings, mostly by Spanish artists including El Greco, Goya, Velázquez and Zurbarán. They became founders of the French association of historic château owners and were pioneers in opening their house to the public. When Carvallo died the art collection was dispersed, but the house and gardens continued to be developed as tourist attractions.

The gardens spread over four terraces in a traditional French style with a sun garden, water garden, ornamental garden and vegetable garden. Each garden is further divided into various themes, such as a love garden, music garden, topiary garden, herb garden and children's garden. A team of 10 gardeners maintains the gardens, which are open all year.

The four great formal gardens at Villandry are among the world's most spectacular gardens

on cobbled track and R again after 200m onto flood dyke (still cobbled). Cycle past le bec du Cher confluence point of Cher with Loire R, and bear L alongside Loire. Continue on flood dyke, passing under motorway bridge and through **La Chapelle-aux-Naux** (29km, 39m) (accommodation).

Pass road bridge that leads over Loire to Langeais and continue on road along flood dyke to **Bréhémont** (35km, 38m) (accommodation, refreshments, camping, cycle shop), where stage ends by church. ◀

Bréhémont (pop 760) is a small village with a large, attractive church. The quay is still actively used by local fishermen in traditional flat-bottomed boats.

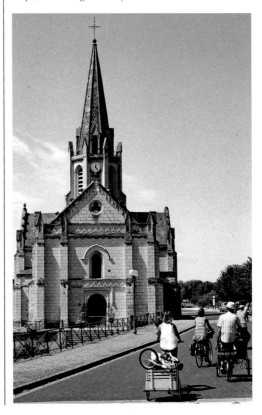

Bréhémont church

STAGE 21
Bréhémont to Saumur

Start	Bréhémont, church (38m)
Finish	Saumur, St Pierre church (37m)
Distance	47.5km
Waymarking	Loire à Vélo

After a long stretch along the Loire flood dyke, the route turns away from the river to avoid the Chinon nuclear power station and picks up the river Vienne, which is then followed back to the Loire. After entering Maine et Cher département at Montsoreau the route climbs onto a low plateau south of the river, eventually descending into the wine-producing town of Saumur. The going is level until Montsoreau, then undulates gently across rolling downland. The riverside limestone cliffs between Montsoreau and Saumur are formed of easily worked white tufa limestone, which has been used extensively for local building stone. The cliffs are riddled with worked-out quarries, many of which have been reused as troglodyte dwellings, mushroom farms or wine cellars.

From quayside in front of **Bréhémont** church, continue W along flood dyke on Ave du 11 Novembre (D16), past **Rupuanne** L (3.5km, 38m) (accommodation), to reach **La Petite Prée**, (6.5km, 37m) where D16 turns L into Rigny-Ussé L accommodation, refreshments, camping).

> The **Château d'Ussé** in Rigny-Ussé (pop 500) is one of the best preserved and prettiest on the Loire. It was the inspiration for Charles Perrault's children's tale *Sleeping Beauty*, and has a wealth of towers and pepper-pot turrets. Originally a medieval defensive castle, it was transformed in the 17th century into a magnificent stately home. The terraces of the formal garden were designed by Maréchal Vauban – better known for designing great military fortifications

– whose daughter married the son of the château's owner, the Marquis de Valentinay, a leading member of Louis XIV's court. The château, which is open to the public, is still a private residence and home of the Duc de Blacas and his family.

Continue (Rue St Martin) for 1km along riverside and where road bears away from river towards St Martin, go ahead on gravel track to continue between fields L and riparian woodland R for 5.5km. Bear L away from river on track winding through small wooded plantations and fields to cross bridge over river Indre into edge of **Le Néman** (13.5km, 36m) (accommodation).

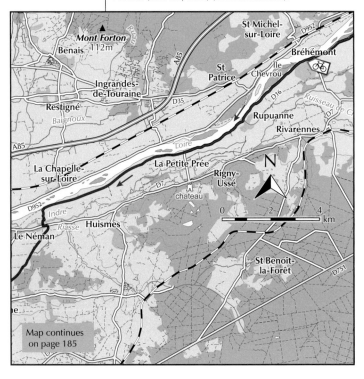

Map continues on page 185

Château d'Ussé was the inspiration for Sleeping Beauty

Turn L (Rue de Val de l'Indre) to reach roundabout. Turn R (Rue de la Perrée) and after 100m fork R (sp Avoine) on country road through fields to reach beginning of Avoine. Continue on Rue de la Tranchée to reach roundabout and fork R (first exit, Rue des Écoles, D118). Continue past church R in centre of **Avoine** (18km, 35m) (accommodation, refreshments). ▶

Turn R (Rue Marcel Vignaud) and after 30m turn L (Rue Perdue) on narrow lane winding L and R between buildings. Continue on cycle track bearing R around car park R and turn L around athletics stadium. Zigzag through fields and cross road. Continue to T-junction and turn L into hamlet of **Beaumont-en-Véron**. Turn R on cycle track beside house 16 and continue through fields to emerge on road head (Rue du Moïté) at beginning of **La Croix**. Continue ahead and turn L at T-junction (Rte des Louzas, D418). Turn R (Rte des Candes) and immediately L (Rue du Bourg) into **Savigny-en-Véron** (21.5km, 33m) (accommodation, refreshments, camping).

Pass square with church L and continue ahead (Rue du Camping) then bear R, passing campsite L. Continue into Rue Basse, passing house with pepper-pot towers R,

Avoine (pop 1800) is a dormitory town for employees of the nearby Chinon nuclear power station.

183

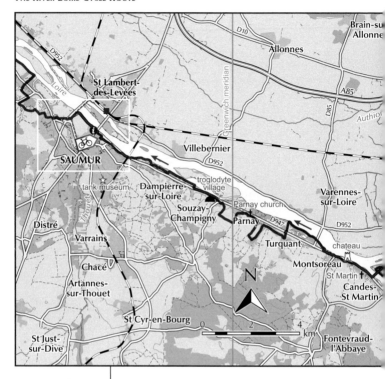

to reach crossroads in hamlet of **Orval**. Turn L through fields and woodland to reach river Vienne.

Turn R along riverbank and continue parallel with river for 2km, then bear R away from river. Turn L at junction of tracks and continue parallel with river under road bridge. Turn R, R and R again to cross bridge over Vienne. Immediately over bridge turn sharply R down-hill onto cycle track along riverbank (Rue du Bac) into **Candes-St Martin** (31km, 35m) (accommodation, refreshments, camping).

The ancient village of **Candes-St Martin** (pop 180) was the site of the death of St Martin, bishop of

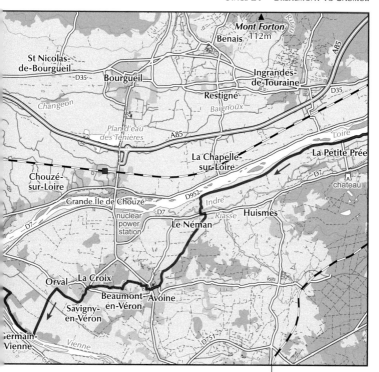

Tours (AD317–AD397). After his death his body was taken upstream to Tours. Legend says that although it was November, flowers bloomed along the river banks, giving rise to the term 'St Martin's summer' referring to a warm period in autumn. The fortified collegiate church, which is dedicated to the saint, has a spectacular castellated north portal.

Bear R through village (Rte de Compostelle), past collegiate church L, to reach roundabout. Fork L (second exit, Rue des Diligences) and bear R (Rue Jehanne d'Arc), ascending a little past château R in centre of **Montsoreau** (32km, 32m) (accommodation, refreshments, camping).

The pretty village of **Montsoreau** (pop 450) grew around a riverside château built in 1455. The village prospered from a medieval market and quay where wine and wheat from local growers were traded and shipped downriver. In the early 19th century, quarrying began of the tufa limestone cliffs that rise behind the village, extracting an attractive building stone. Since the galleries opened by the quarrymen were exhausted of stone, the tunnels have been used to cultivate many varieties of mushrooms and fungi for high-quality restaurants. Another series of galleries are used as a cooperative wine market, where visitors can sample and purchase a large variety of wines from the Loire Valley.

Continue through village on Rue du Port au Vin, descending to riverside. Bear L (Quai Philippe de Commines) and opposite house 7 drop down R through barriers onto quayside. Fork R (initially cobbled) then cross small bridge and turn L and R around tennis courts to emerge beside main road with Maison du Parc offices of regional natural park L and cyclists' rest place R. Continue below cliffs of limestone tufa with quarry galleries and tunnels cut into them. Immediately after campsite R, turn R on gravel track between yew hedges. Follow this to reach river and turn L along riverbank, passing under road bridge and continuing for 2km.

Turn L away from river on quiet road to reach roundabout. Follow cycle track circling anti-clockwise through small vineyard beside roundabout to continue on road opposite (Rue des Martyrs, sp Turquant, cycle track R) into beginning of **Turquant** (35.5km, 39m) (accommodation, refreshments).

Turn R (Pl St Aubin) after parish church then bear R around back of church into Rue de la Mairie. Continue into Rue du Château Gaillard, winding beside houses built into cliffs L, and fork R downhill into Rue des Ducs d'Anjou out of village. Turn L at crossroads (Rue Valbrun), ascending through wine-producing village of **Parnay** (accommodation, refreshments).

Turquant is a wine-producing village in Saumur AC

At T-junction turn R (Rte des Vins), ascending out of village. Before top of hill, turn R (Ch de Beniquet), winding through vineyards. Where road ends continue ahead on gravel track, bearing L along clifftop. Pass Parnay church R and turn R (La Haute Rue), winding downhill into detached part of Parnay. Fork L (Rue Antoine Cristal) uphill and at end of village, turn R on road through more vines. ▶

Turn R (Rue Jean Brevet) downhill, passing church R, then fork L (Ch des Écoliers). Go ahead over crossroads into narrow lane (still Ch des Écoliers), passing primary school R. Turn L into Parcours Troglodytique and R to wind through underground village in **Souzay-Champigny** (41.5km, 34m). ▶

At end of underground village, turn L briefly uphill then downhill. Bear L onto cycle track beside Rue de Château, passing houses L built into cliff face. Pass through more underground dwellings then turn R, dropping down steeply to reach main road. Cross main road and turn L on cycle track beside road to reach beginning of **Dampierre-sur-Loire** (accommodation, refreshments).

Follow cycle track bearing R away from road, then zigzag L and R past car park. At end of car park, zigzag L and R again onto quiet road past caravan park L. Bear

At this point route crosses Greenwich meridian and moves from the Eastern into the Western hemisphere.

The limestone cliffs below Souzay-Champigny are riddled with caves. These contain a spectacular underground village with underground streets and underground houses.

Caves at Souzay-Champigny contain a troglodyte village with underground streets and dwellings

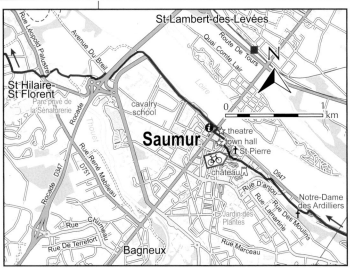

L onto gravel track beside Loire and follow this for 3km, winding through riparian woodland.

Emerge beside main road and turn R under railway bridge (cycle track R). Opposite domed Notre-Dame des Ardilliers church, turn L across road and turn R past front of church into Pl Notre-Dame des Ardilliers. Continue into Rue Rabelais (cycle lane L) then into Rue Joachim du Bellay. Turn L (Rue de la Croix du Vigneau), then bear R on Rue Jean Jaurès and continue into Rue Fourrier, passing below château L with troglodyte caves cut into hillside.

Continue on pedestrianised Rue Haute St Pierre, passing St Pierre church R to reach shady Pl St Pierre in centre of **Saumur** (47.5km, 37m) (accommodation, refreshments, camping, tourist office, cycle shop, station).

SAUMUR

The wine-producing town of Saumur (pop 28,500) is dominated by its château, which is built of creamy coloured local tufa limestone and stands on a small hill above the town centre. Originally a military castle, it was transformed in the late 14th century into a sumptuous palace for the Duke of Anjou, the brother of King Charles V. Later it became the home of the governor of Saumur. During the Wars of Religion, Saumur was a Protestant stronghold, and to repel Catholic forces the château was fortified with defensive bastions that predated Vauban by 100 years. Later it became a prison and POW camp for British prisoners during the Napoleonic Wars. From 1814 to 1889 it was a barracks and armoury. Restoration began in 1906 and the château nowadays houses museums dedicated to decorative arts, equestrianism and miniature figurines.

Saumur has a long equestrian history, which started in 1763 when a cavalry training school was established in barracks east of the town centre. After 1830 this became the main riding academy for officers of the French cavalry, with an outdoor riding arena and an indoor training hall. After the Second World War, decline in military use of horses led to Saumur becoming a centre for motorised armoured forces, and the town houses the French national tank museum. Saumur has, however, retained its position as the French centre of excellence for horsemanship. The Cadre Noir display team is based here and the training facilities are used by French elite international riders.

STAGE 22
Saumur to Angers

Start	Saumur, St Pierre church (37m)
Finish	Les Ponts-de-Cé church (Angers) (20m)
Distance	50km (58km to Angers centre)
Waymarking	Loire à Vélo

From Saumur the route starts south of the Loire, mostly on riverside roads below the cliffs that line the valley, with two short climbs onto the rolling downland above these cliffs. The river is crossed to St Mathurin-sur-Loire, and the route is then completely level, winding through highly fertile farmland on quiet roads and passing a series of small agricultural hamlets. A final stretch on a riverside flood dyke brings the stage to an end at Les Ponts-de-Cé, 5km south of the historic city of Angers. An alternative route through the Trélazé slate quarries allows you to visit Angers.

From Pl St Pierre in centre of **Saumur**, head N on Rue de la Tonnelle, forking R to reach Quai Mayaud on Loire riverside. Turn L on contra-flow cycle lane through Pl de la Republique, passing town hall L. Continue into Rue Molière, past theatre R and turn R (Pl de la Bilange) to reach roundabout. Turn L (Quai Carnot, third exit) beside Loire, passing tourist office, and continue ahead at next roundabout. Follow cycle track beside Bvd Henri Dunant, passing cavalry school and barracks L.

Where road turns away from river, continue along riverbank (Ch de Halage des Huraudieres) for 100m then bear L, parallel with motorway. At end turn R (Ave de Breil) under bridge then turn immediately L, parallel with motorway slip road. Bear R at roundabout (first exit) and after 20m turn L across road and through barrier onto cycle track through parkland.

Bear R to continue alongside river Thouet, then L to cross river over weirs and ruined lock. Turn L along boardwalk then R on gravel track soon forking R uphill. Go ahead over main road and bear R at T-junction (Rue de l'Abbaye) through **St Hilaire-St Florent** (3km, 38m) (accommodation, refreshments, camping).

Cycle uphill past parish church L to reach small roundabout with tree in middle and turn R (Rue des Sables). Follow road curving L past cemetery L then bearing R to reach T-junction. Turn L (Rue du Porteau) and after 80m fork R (Ch des Saurondes). Continue downhill through fields used to graze horses from national riding academy, then bear R and R again (Rue de la Petite Fontaine).

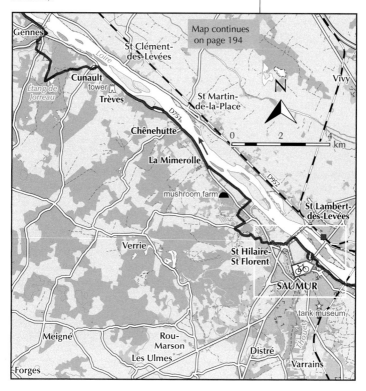

Map continues on page 194

Notre-Dame des Tuffeaux church in Chênehutte

To visit a mushroom museum and farm in the cliffside caves, turn L along the main road for 500m.

La Cave aux Moines, an underground mushroom farm on the left in Préban, can be visited.

Continue downhill and turn L after house 76 (Ch de Beauchêne). Fork L on gravel track ascending beside golf course L and turn R at T-junction. Emerge on road and follow this downhill through built-up area and continue across main road through fields to reach Loire. ◄ Bear L beside river for 2.25km, then follow track L to reach main road. Turn R onto cycle track beside road (Rte des Gennes, D751) through hamlet of **La Mimerolle** (9.5km, 28m) (camping).

Continue on cycle lane beside main road, with cliffs rising L and river R, through **Chênehutte** (10.5km, 31m) (accommodation, refreshments). Road continues through St Jean, where cycle track bears R away from road winding through hamlet, then returns to roadside to reach Préban (accommodation, refreshments). ◄ Continue through **Trèves** (14km, 26m) (accommodation) into **Cunault** (15km, 30m) (accommodation, refreshments).

The three villages of **Chênehutte-Trèves-Cunault** (pop 1000) merged in 1974 to form one long community along the riverside. The main points of interest are the ruins and tower of Trèves Castle.

Built originally as a defensive castle during the Norman period (11th century), it saw action during the Hundred Years' War. As it was an English stronghold, one fanciful French novel claims it to be the birthplace of Arthurian hero Lancelot. The castle was remodelled as a residential building in the 15th century and extended in the 17th. It was pulled down in 1750, with only the tower remaining intact. Inside are huge vaulted rooms, bare and deserted, with kitchens in the basement and dungeons in the lowest level.

Fork L in village (D213, sp Doué), past church L, and turn L at crossroads (Rue Notre-Dame). After 80m, fork R uphill (Rue du Cadran), winding through village on narrow lane. At end bear R then turn L and R (Rue de la Sablière). Continue ascending past housing development L, then fork L and follow narrow road out of village through barrier into woods.

Turn R at main road, then after 40m turn L to descend through woods past **Étang de Jorreau lake** L. Turn sharply R by car park, continuing downhill, and

Étang de Jorreau lake

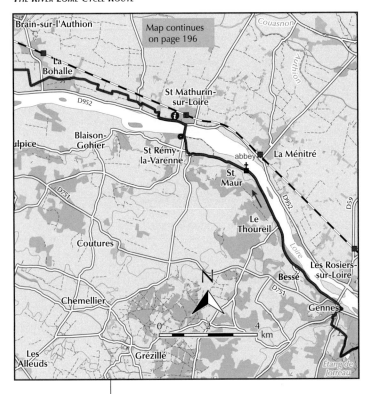

Brain-sur-l'Authion

Map continues
on page 196

La Bohalle

St Mathurin-
sur-Loire

D952

Blaison-
Gohier

ulpice

St Rémy-
la-Varenne

abbey

La Ménitré

St Maur

D751

Le Thoureil

D952

Loire

D59

Coutures

Les Rosiers-
sur-Loire

N

Bessé

Chemellier

D751

Gennes

0   2   4
                km

Les Alleuds

Grézillé

Étang de Jorreau

turn L at T-junction (Rue du Clos Baujon) into beginning of Gennes. At mini-roundabout, fork L (second exit) and continue ahead (Ave de l'Amphithéâtre, D70) over second (full-size) roundabout on cycle track R of road. Turn R downhill on cycle track through fields. At bottom of hill cross small bridge then bear L and turn R (Ch du Mardron) to cross second bridge. Turn R (Sq du Marais), then L and R (Rue de l'Ancienne Mairie) in centre of **Gennes** (20km, 30m) (accommodation, refreshments, camping).

Fork L (Rue de la République) and at end bear R ahead across sidestreet onto short cobbled path that passes to R of roundabout. Cross next exit from roundabout onto cycle track between bushes and follow this, bearing R then L downhill away from road. After 125m bear sharply L and go ahead over crossroads past campsite R. Cross next road onto Rte du Thoureil (D132) and follow this past swimming pool R out of town with cliffs rising L and Loire R.

Continue past **Bessé** (22.5km, 28m) (accommodation, refreshments) and follow riverbank road (Quai des Mariniers) through **Le Thoureil** (24.5km, 29m) (accommodation, refreshments) and **St Maur** (27km, 26m) (accommodation, refreshments).

> The **Abbaye St Maur** was first established as a Benedictine abbey in the sixth century. Destroyed by the Normans, it was rebuilt and fortified during the Hundred Years' War. The current building dates from the 17th century.

Continue on Rue St Jean de l'Isle to beginning of St Rémy-la Varenne and fork R (Rue du Ban). At end turn R into square in centre of **St Rémy-la-Varenne** (30km, 29m) (accommodation, refreshments).

Pass church and turn immediately R. Bear L through car park, then turn R on gravel track, passing sports field R. At end bear R on cycle track to reach river. Turn L under bridge, then immediately L and L again over Loire bridge (D55) to reach roundabout. Turn L (second exit, D952) into **St Mathurin-sur-Loire** (31.5km, 26m) (accommodation, refreshments, camping, tourist office, station).

Pass through town on main road (Levée du Roi René) using cycle lane R and just before end of town sign, turn R on quiet road into Grande Rue hamlet. Turn L opposite house 14 (Ch du Vieil Errault) and continue through fields to La Marsaulaye hamlet.

Turn L at T-junction, then after 100m turn R at next T-junction. Fork L to continue between fields into Le Voisinay. Turn R, then follow road bearing L through hamlet and ahead through fields. At T-junction turn L, and after 100m turn R (Ch de la Messagerie). Continue through fields to reach T-junction in Le Coureau. Turn R

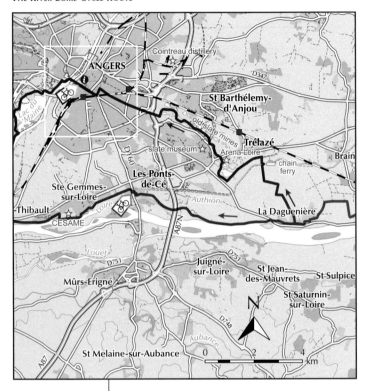

through hamlet and after 200m turn L (Rue des Ruettes) through fields. Go ahead over crossroads (Rue de Carrefour), then bear L into **La Bohalle** (37.5km, 19m) (accommodation, station).

Turn R at crossroads (Rue le Bas Chemin), then go ahead through village, passing chapel R. Continue on quiet country road past school L. Go ahead over crossroads (Rue Cailleteau) through La Chesnaie.

After 500m, turn R (Ch des Prés) through fields to reach T-junction. Turn L (Rue de la Daguenière) and just after Parc d'Activité du Pré Lellie L, turn L (Rue de Chanay) into beginning of Villeneuve la Croix. Fork R beside large wooden cross (Rue de Villeneuve). Turn L at T-junction (Rue du Val d'Authion) and after 70m turn R (Rue St Laud). Turn L at crossroads (Rue du Grand Richelieu) then R at T-junction (Rue Ligérienne) into centre of **La Daguenière** (42.5km, 22m) (accommodation, refreshments).

> **La Daguenière** (pop 1300) is the centre of a highly fertile agricultural and horticultural area, with crops, flowers and seeds growing on soils of silt brought down by the Loire in past times when the river experienced regular flooding.

Alternative route via Angers
Turn R beside house 92 (sp Gare d'Angers par les Ardoisières) into Pl de l'Église, then dog-leg L and R in front of church and follow Rue du Stade out of village past sports club L. Turn L at T-junction, then fork R (Rue de la Grange) and turn R on quiet road through fields to reach another T-junction. Turn L and after 200m R, continuing through fields to crossroads. Turn L, then R at next T-junction and continue over drainage canal. Zigzag R and L over flood dyke to reach ferry ramp and use **chain ferry** to cross river Authion (46.5km, 18m). ▶

The self-operated Bac du Chevalerie chain ferry is available from late Mar to mid Nov, 0830–1930.

A self-operated chain ferry is used to cross the river Authion

Levée Napoléon was constructed in 1856 under the orders of Napoléon III after a flood inundated the slate quarries at Trélazé trapping 2000 miners.

Continue ahead away from river for 300m, then turn L at crossing of tracks onto cycle track along Levée Napoléon flood dyke. ◀ Pass Le Puit de Napoléon lake R and turn R on cycle track winding through scrubland. Fork R and just before car park for Arena Loire sports hall turn L to continue on cycle track through Parc des Ardoisières.

> The **Trélazé Ardoisières**, which spread over a large area between Trélazé and St Barthélemy-d'Anjou, are former slate quarries that first opened in 1406. Originally all slate was extracted from open pits until the first underground mine opened in 1838. As all the easily reached slate was exhausted, so more activity moved underground, with the last open quarry closing in 1899. Peak production was reached in 1911, but decline set in after the Second World War as demand for natural slate fell. The last mine closed in 2014 when all the affordably mined stone was exhausted. When they closed, they were the last operational slate quarries in France. Eight old mine shafts, tailings mounds of mine waste and several flooded pits remain. There is a museum which explains the history of local slate mining.

Cross bridge over main road, then follow track bending sharply L to reach road. Turn R (Rue Ambroise Croizat) using cycle lane R, then bear R at T-junction. Continue between industrial estate L and derelict slate workings R to roundabout. Take first exit (D117, sp Toutes Directions) on cycle track beside slate waste tip R. At next roundabout turn L across first exit road then go ahead through barriers on cycle track between first and second exits. Follow this, winding through old slate workings and passing two flooded quarries, both R. Dog-leg L and R over staggered crossing, then fork L and pass under road bridge. Pass allotments L, then bear L to reach road. Turn R (Rue Pierre et Marie Curie) then after 300m, fork R (Rue du 8 Mai 1945) using cycle track R. Continue to pedestrian crossing, then cross road and turn back on other side for short distance before forking R on cycle track winding through La Paperie mine workings (53.5km, 29m).

Follow cycle track bearing L opposite entrance to Villechien compost producing plant. Emerge beside road (Rue de la Paperie) and continue to roundabout. Turn R (first exit, Rue St Léonard) then follow this under motorway and ahead across junction with two mini-roundabouts. Pass Raymond Kopa stadium (Angers FC) L and go ahead over dual carriageway. Continue for 1km, passing over railway bridge into Rue Célestine-Port to reach five-way junction (Pl du Lycée). Turn sharply L (Rue Paul Langevin) past school L, then at next crossroads turn R (Rue Bressigny) and continue to reach dual carriageway with tram tracks in the middle. Turn L (Rue du Haras),

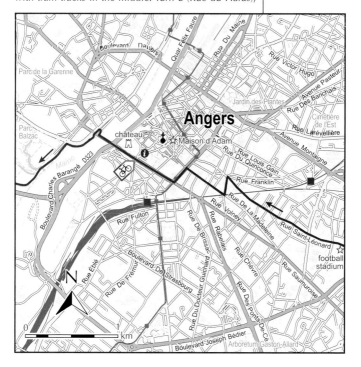

ANGERS

Angers castle walls (photo Christine Gordon)

Angers (urban pop 240,000) sits beside the river Maine 8km above its confluence with the Loire. As the capital of Anjou, it was the cradle of the Plantagenet dynasty that ruled over England and western France from the 12th to 15th centuries. The well-preserved medieval castle, which has 600m of surrounding walls with 17 bastions, saw action during the Hundred Years' War (1347–1453) when Anjou was fought over by the English and French. Inside the castle, the most famous work of art is the Apocalypse tapestry (1377). This stretches for over 80m and depicts the story of the Revelation of St John. Displayed for many years in the city's cathedral, it was looted during the Revolution and cut into many pieces which were used for a multiplicity of purposes including horse blankets and frost covers for orange trees. By 1848 many of the parts had been recovered and preservation began. Since 1954 it has been on display in a purpose-built gallery in the castle. The city's old quarter has many medieval houses, including the half-timbered Maison d'Adam. St Barthélemy-d'Anjou, in the eastern suburbs of Angers, is the site of a distillery producing the orange-flavoured liqueur Cointreau.

then turn R at next crossroads (Bvd du Roi René, sp Rennes). Follow this to reach road junction in centre of **Angers** (58km, 38m) (accommodation, refreshments, YH, camping, tourist office, cycle shop, station), with statue of Roi René in middle of road and walls of Château Angers ahead.

Main route continues
Cycle ahead through village to reach roundabout surrounded by square stone wall. Turn R before this wall and follow cycle track around outside of roundabout. Cross main road and turn R on cycle track L of road (D952). After 100m, fork L on quiet road along flood dyke. Continue for 6km, passing small Château de Belle Poule R and going under motorway to reach beginning of Les Ponts-de-Cé.

Drop down R off flood dyke then bear R (Rue Kléber), and after 75m turn L (Rue Louis Blon). ▶ Turn L after parish church (Rue Marceau) to reach main road by St Aubin church in middle of **Les Ponts-de-Cé** (50km, 20m) (accommodation, refreshments, camping, cycle shop).

Rue Louis Blon is a one-way street with a contra-flow cycle lane.

STAGE 23
Angers to Montjean-sur-Loire

Start	Les Ponts-de-Cé church (Angers) (20m)
Finish	Montjean-sur-Loire, bridge (12m)
Distance	36.5km (37.5km from Angers centre)
Waymarking	Loire à Vélo

Starting north of the Loire, this generally flat stage mostly follows flood dykes and quiet riverside roads, with two short climbs and descents on and off a low ridge bounding the river. The last 11km traverse an island between two arms of the river.

Route from Angers

If you've visited **Angers**, you do not have retrace your route. From statue of Roi René beside Château Angers, cycle NW (Bvd de Général de Gaulle), crossing Pont de la Basse Chaîne bridge over river Maine. At end of bridge, fork R downhill then turn sharply L (Bvd du Bon Pasteur), back under bridge. ◄ After 150m bear L across road to join cycle track L. Follow this, first curving R above riverside terracing then bearing L onto gravel cycle track through gardens parallel with Maine L. Follow track bearing R and pass under motorway, then bear R to circle **Lac du Maine** L in anti-clockwise direction. Pass pyramid-shaped water sports club L and bear L to pass campsite R (camping). Where track divides beside park maintenance depot, take gravel fork, R. Continue to reach riverbank and turn R along riverside track, passing under footbridge. Emerge onto quiet road (Quai de la Noé) and continue under railway bridge to reach **Bouchemaine** (8km, 20m) (accommodation, refreshments, camping, cycle shop). Turn sharply L on gravel track towards river, re-joining main route.

Major road works associated with a new tram line have disrupted the route after crossing the river Maine. Look out for diversions.

Main route

From outside St Aubin Church in **Les Ponts-de-Cé**, cycle W for 50m on Passage Joseph Gilbert. Turn first R (Rue du Pochetet). Dog-leg L and R across quayside road and cross bridge over river Authion. Turn L onto cycle track parallel with river for 2km, then pass through barrier and turn R onto road (Levée de L'Authion) into **Ste Gemmes-sur-Loire** (2.5km, 22m) (camping).

After 125m, fork L (Promenade de Belle Rive) on narrow road that bypasses town centre. Where this turns R, turn L towards river on gravel road and bear R on cycle track along riverbank, passing high walls of **CESAME** psychiatric hospital R. Follow track, bearing R through

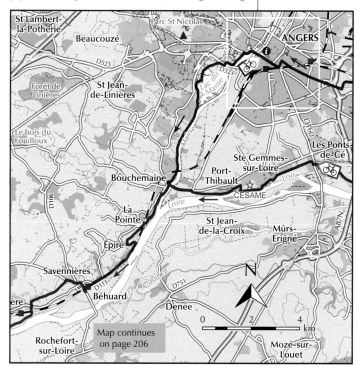

Map continues on page 206

barrier beside walls to reach roundabout. Turn L (Rte de Port Thibault, third exit) using cycle lane R and continue through **Port-Thibault**.

At end of village, bear L to continue parallel with river. Turn R at T-junction on cycle track L, then follow cycle track bearing L beside roundabout and continue beside main road (D112). At mini-roundabout, cross to R of road and continue on suspension bridge over river Maine to reach roundabout in **Bouchemaine** (7km, 20m) (accommodation, refreshments, camping, cycle shop). ◄ Turn R (first exit) and immediately R (Quai de la Noé), then turn R again on gravel track towards river, joining route via Angers.

The busy road over the bridge is narrow with no cycle lane.

Combined route continues

Bear R under bridge and continue past camper van park R. Turn R away from river for 75m and just before main road, turn sharply L back towards river. Cross slipway and continue on gravel track beside river. Emerge onto quiet road (Quai de Port Boulet) and fork R into **La Pointe** (9km, 25m) (accommodation, refreshments).

Fork L in village into narrow one-way street (Rue du Port-Boulet) with contra-flow cycling permitted. Turn R at T-junction (Rue des Pivins) and turn first L (Rue de la Grenouille). At end, turn R uphill (Rue Croix-Vert) and L at T-junction (Rue des Saulniers), winding through village. Fork R at road junction, passing under railway bridge and turning immediately L to ascend steeply, parallel with railway (Rte de la Croix Picot). Ascend steadily through open country to reach **Épiré** (10.5km, 50m) (accommodation, refreshments).

Turn L beside stone cross at beginning of village and follow road winding downhill through trees and passing under railway to riverbank. Turn R between railway and Loire and continue for 3km, eventually following railway away from river past station R. Turn immediately L and L again to follow main road (D106) under bridge. Where road turns L, continue ahead (Rue de la Motte) into **Savennières** (14.5km, 25m) (accommodation, refreshments, station).

St Pierre et St Romain Romanesque church in Savennières

Savennières (pop 1350) is a small wine-producing town in the Anjou wine region with three recognised AC vineyards. Chenin blanc grapes are used to produce dry white wines with relatively high acidity that mature well with age. The leading vineyard, Coulée de Serrant, was first planted by Cistercian monks in 1130. Its output is regarded as one of the world's top dry white wines. The most significant building is the Romanesque church of St Pierre et St Romain, built between the 10th and 12th centuries with an attractive portico and banded brickwork.

Bear L in front of church (Rue Duboys d'Angers), then turn first R (Rue Monsallier). Turn L beside house 11 (Rue Louis et Maurice Frouin) to reach T-junction and turn R (Rue du Beau Soleil) uphill. Turn L beside house 15 (Rue de la Pierre de Coulaine) and ascend gently out

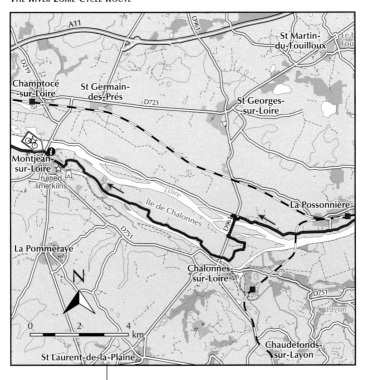

of village. Turn L again, after house 29, (Ch de l'Aiglerie) and continue ascending through open country. Go ahead at crossroads and onto cycle track across plateau through vineyards. Emerge onto quiet road (Ch de la Hutte) and continue on Rue de Bel Air, starting to descend. Turn L beside house 9 along narrow street (Rue du Guet), descending through **La Possonnière** (17.5km, 29m) (accommodation, refreshments, camping, station). ◀

This turn is easy to miss.

Pass church L and continue downhill on Rue du Four à Ban. Turn R at T-junction (Rue du Prieuré) and after 50m turn L (Bvd du Port). Continue descending under railway bridge and fork R on cycle track, bearing R parallel with river. After 1.3km turn R up cobbled ramp and L to join road (D210) along top of flood dyke. Continue under railway bridge and past Le Port Girault hamlet (22.5km, 14m) (accommodation).

At end of hamlet, fork L off flood dyke and follow winding gravel track to riverbank. Pass under road bridge and after 130m turn R and R again to reach road. Turn R onto road and R (D961, sp Chalonnes) to cross main arm of Loire on girder bridge using cycle track R. Continue across second bridge (over Cordez arm) and turn R and R again to pass under bridge. Turn R again and L past Cordez farm on track parallel with river. ▶

After 750m, turn R on gravel track winding through Le Chapeau hamlet. Turn R at T-junction, and after 400m turn L through fields. Turn R at T-junction, and just before Chalonnes suspension bridge bear L through barriers on cycle track under bridge (27km, 14m) (refreshments). ▶

Continue beside river to reach T-junction and turn L through Le Fremoir hamlet. Opposite Le Bordage farm, turn L into La Basse Île (31.5km, 13m) (refreshments). At end of village bear L to reach river and continue along riverbank. At tiny La Queue de l'Île hamlet, bear R away from river and turn L at T-junction. Fork L, and after 150m fork R onto girder bridge and cross minor branch of Loire. Turn R along riverside road (Quai Monseigneur Provost), passing ruins of old lime kilns L, to reach end of suspension bridge in **Montjean-sur-Loire** (36.5km, 12m) (accommodation, refreshments, camping, tourist office).

From here to stage end at Montjean-sur-Loire, route is along Île de Chalonnes island between two branches of Loire.

To visit Chalonnes-sur-Loire (accommodation, refreshments, cycle shop, station), turn L over the bridge.

MONTJEAN-SUR-LOIRE

The post-industrial town of Montjean-sur-Loire (pop 3100) is on the site of a Norman castle which was rebuilt as a Franciscan convent in 1493. This castle (originally known as Bellevue and now called Le Fief des Cordelier) has recently been restored as a luxury hotel. By the 19th century the town had become an important port, with many inhabitants employed as sailors and an estimated 6000 boats passing through in 1838. The coming of the railway in 1850 took over much of this trade and by 1900 only 60 boats remained, mostly carrying lime to England. A replica barge, La Gabare du Montjeannaise, stands in Cap Loire discovery park. It used to operate on

Montjean-sur-Loire bridge was rebuilt in 1948

the river until health and safety regulations prevented it from carrying passengers. Industrial development centred around lime kilns and coal mined to fire these kilns. Output peaked in 1891 when 23 lime kilns were in operation, but subsequently declined. The last kiln closed in 1962.

The Loire bridge was destroyed twice during the Second World War; once by the Germans in 1940 who then rebuilt it, and again by the Americans on D-day in 1944. The current bridge opened in 1948.

STAGE 24
Montjean-sur-Loire to Ancenis

Start	Montjean-sur-Loire, bridge (12m)
Finish	Ancenis, château (13m)
Distance	28.5km
Waymarking	Loire à Vélo

This short and completely flat stage mostly uses flood dykes and field paths to enter the Muscadet wine-producing region.

From S end of Loire bridge in **Montjean-sur-Loire**, cycle W along Quai des Mariniers (D210), parallel with Loire. Pass campsite L and continue on road along flood dyke to reach Le Port de Ingrandes (4.5km, 13m) (accommodation, refreshments, camping). ▸

Go ahead over crossroads and continue along dyke-top road past Cul de Bœuf to reach beginning of St Florent-le-Vieil. Cross river Thau and drop down R off flood dyke onto gravel cycle track beside river (Promenade Julien Gracq). Continue to reach riverside parking area (Quai de la Loire) in **St Florent-le-Vieil** (13km, 15m) (accommodation, refreshments, camping, tourist office, station).

Bear R on cobbled ramp to pass under St Florent bridge and continue along riverbank cycle track, passing below abbey, castle and memorial column on clifftop L. ▸ Turn L away from river at Les Lusses to reach T-junction. Turn R (Rue du Vieux Bourg), passing huge Notre-Dame basilica L in Le Vieux Bourg (15km, 13m) (refreshments).

Turn R at mini-roundabout (Rue du l'Èvre, D751) and cross stone bridge over river Èvre. Immediately after

To visit the small town of Ingrandes (accommodation, refreshments, station), turn R across the Loire bridge.

Only the abbey is visible from the track.

ST FLORENT-LE-VIEIL

The medieval centre of St Florent-le-Vieil (pop 2800) sits on Mont-Glonne, a small bluff beside the Loire. Here St Florent, a fourth-century Christian hermit, established a church which developed into an abbey. Destroyed by the Vikings (AD853), it was rebuilt and fortified in the 11th century with walls that also encircled the small town that had grown up around the abbey – walls that were demolished after the town was captured (1581) during the Wars of Religion. Disaster struck the town following the Revolution, when during the War in the Vendée (1793) the local population rose up against the republican government in a protest over conscription into the army. Retribution was brutal; over 1000 residents were slaughtered and the town burnt down with only one house surviving. After the restoration of the monarchy this event was commemorated with a memorial column erected by the Duchess of Angoulême, daughter of Louis XVI. In the lower town, the small Tour de la Gabelle beside the bridge was used by customs officials to collect salt tax from merchants crossing the Loire.

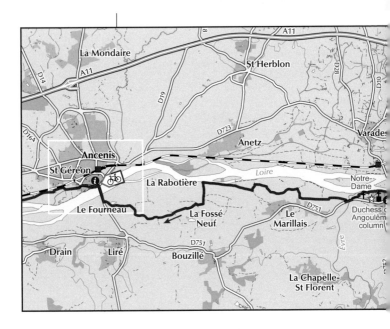

St Florent-le-Vieil abbey stands on Mont-Glonne hill overlooking the Loire

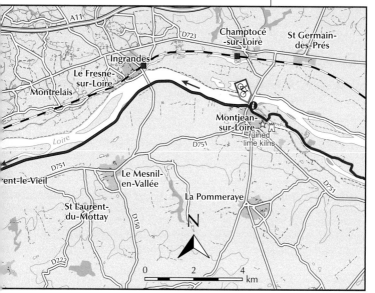

bridge join cycle track R and follow this, bearing R. Turn R onto quiet road and follow this curving L through fields.

After 2km, with large farm L, turn R at crossroads and then L at T-junction. Continue winding through fields, passing two farms, and after 1.2km fork R. At T-junction, where track R is unsurfaced, turn L and after 300m follow road turning sharply R. Pass through La Loge en Vallée hamlet to reach T-junction. Turn R, passing campsite L and running beside river R. Pass through Les Babins and at next road junction, on edge of **La Rabotière**, turn L away from river (sp Bouzillé).

Continue through fields, and just before stone bridge on edge of **La Fossé Neuf** (23km, 8m) (accommodation) turn R on gravel track to bypass village. Fork L by car park past ornamental lakes L and continue winding through fields. Bear R at track junction then emerge on road and continue to reach T-junction. Turn R, then after 500m bear L past active quarry behind trees R. Continue on Les Garennes into **Le Fourneau** (28km, 11m) (refreshments).

Emerge on road serving chalk quarries and turn L to reach main road. Turn R (D763) and cross suspension bridge over Loire into **Ancenis** (28.5km, 13m) (accommodation, refreshments, camping, tourist office, station).

Ancenis (pop 7650) was established in AD984 by the Bretons on what was at the time an island in the Loire, with the objective of defending the border between Brittany and Anjou. Boulevards that surround the town centre follow the route of the original stream that encircled the town. The old castle, which is approached over a drawbridge and was rebuilt as a Renaissance palace in the 15th century, is not open to visitors. The Ursuline convent on the edge of town, nowadays known as the 'Rohan district', was built in 1642. After being suppressed during the Revolution it became a military hospital and then a barracks until 1982. The site has been redeveloped for offices and housing, removing many 19th-century additions and restoring the monastic buildings – including the chapel, which is now an art gallery.

Ancenis castle with drawbridge between two towers

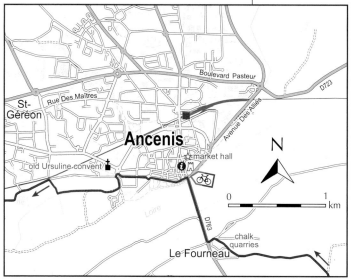

213

STAGE 25

Ancenis to Nantes

Start	Ancenis, château (13m)
Finish	Nantes, Général Audibert bridge (7m)
Distance	39km
Waymarking	Loire à Vélo

Between Ancenis and Nantes the Loire passes through a gorge with cliffs rising steeply beside the river's north bank. There has been a problem with rockfall and the route avoids this by crossing the river to use newly constructed cycle tracks winding through fields on the south bank between Oudon and Mauves. After crossing back to the north bank, the route follows a traffic-free route into Nantes.

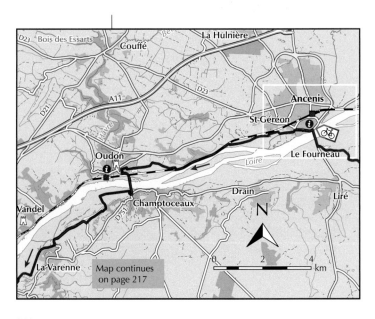

Map continues on page 217

From mini-roundabout at end of bridge in front of châ-teau in **Ancenis**, follow Bvd Joubert W. After 100m join cycle track L between road and riverside gardens. Pass roundabout and continue ahead beside Bvd de Kirkham R. Turn L in front of modern Théâtre Quartier Libre and immediately L again at mini-roundabout (Impasse de l'Île Mouchet, second exit). Pass football stadium entrance R and turn R through barriers onto gravel track. Go ahead over crossing of tracks, then turn R at next junction. At end turn L beside railway bridge, then fork L at road junction and turn R on quiet tree-lined road. After 1.7km, turn R at T-junction then turn L on gravel track beside railway line. Follow this through barriers with railway R and Loire L, and after 2.5km turn R under railway bridge. After 100m bear L by Mont-Piron farm, then fork L to continue through fields and reach road at T-junction.

Turn L and follow road past plan d'eau reservoir and sports ground (both L) to roundabout. Turn L (Rue du Chêne) and at end turn L to reach T-junction in **Oudon** (9km, 10m) (accommodation, refreshments, camping, tourist office, station).

La Garde de la Tour sculpture in front of Oudon castle

Oudon (pop 3850) developed around an 11th-century medi-eval defensive castle. This was rebuilt with a new main tower in 1392, and this tower remains a dominant feature of the town. Since 1996 Oudon has hosted a biennial festival of outdoor sculpture, in which leading inter-national sculptors are invited to create works of art around the town. Over the years many have remained in place and now form an urban sculpture walk.

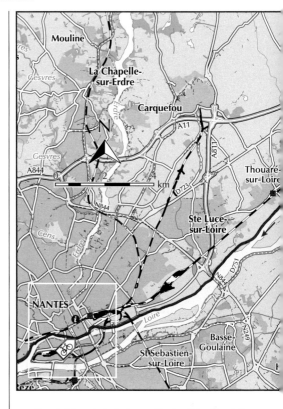

Turn L (Rue de la Loire, sp Toutes Directions) then R at mini-roundabout to reach junction with main road. Turn L (sp Champtoceaux, D751C) then pass over railway bridge and continue on bridge across Loire. Just before next road junction (refreshments), turn sharply R on cycle track back towards river then turn L through barriers onto gravel cycle track winding between fields L and riparian woodland R. After 1.3km, bear L away from river then turn L at T-junction and continue ahead through La Bridonnière hamlet (cycle shop). Turn R at T-junction then continue past bridge R that leads to a golf course on L'Île

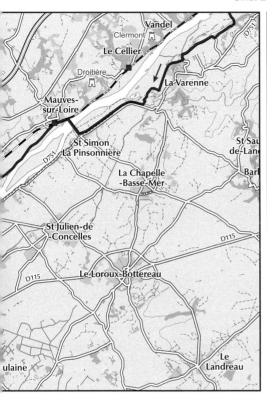

d'Or island to reach beginning of **La Varenne** (15.5km, 10m) (camping).

Turn R, passing below village on hillside L and continue past campsite and sports field (both L) into open country. Turn R at T-junction then follow winding road dog-legging L and R through L'Aireau hamlet (accommodation, refreshments). Just before house 8, turn L onto gravel cycle track winding through fields and crossing river Divatte. Bear R beside main road (D751, on top of flood dyke) then follow cycle track away from road, passing farm L and winding along river bank for short distance before returning to main road. Continue beside road for 2.5km, passing through area of intensive vegetable cultivation. Just before Pont du Mauves bridge over Loire, turn sharply L up to road and then R along top of flood dyke to roundabout in **St Simon La Pinsonnière** (21.5km, 8m) (refreshments).

Turn R (sp Mauves, D31, first exit) and cross bridges over Divatte and Loire using cycle track R. At end of bridge follow cycle track bearing R then turn R towards river and follow cobbled track under bridge. After 300m, pass turn R that leads under main road and railway to **Mauves-sur-Loire** (23km, 5m) (accommodation, refreshments, cycle shop, station).

> **Mauves-sur-Loire** (pop 3250) was a Gallo-Roman resort town for affluent inhabitants of the region with a temple, theatre and baths. Nowadays it is a dormitory town for Nantes with a growing population.

To visit Thouaré (accommodation, refreshments, cycle shop, station), continue ahead up to bridge and turn R on main road to reach the town centre after 600m.

Bear R to follow cycle track beside main road, passing station R, and follow this curving L away from railway to emerge on quiet country road (Ch de la Sauternelle) with marshy foreshore L and intensive vegetable cultivation R. After 4.5km, bear L on cycle track beside road to pass under girder bridge carrying road into **Thouaré-sur-Loire** (28km, 5m). ◄

Re-join road and continue ahead. Where road turns R, continue ahead on cycle track (Promenade de Loire). Pass Belle Rivière R (camping) and emerge onto quiet road beside aggregates quay (Allée Robert Cheval). Go ahead over mini-roundabout (Promenade de Bellevue) and pass through riverside community of Bellevue (32km, 5m) (accommodation, refreshments).

Bear L on cycle track under motorway. Re-join road and where this ends continue ahead through barriers, following cycle track for 2km past large Gypsy caravan park R. Emerge on road, then join cycle track beside riverside road (Ch des Bateliers). Bear L to bypass roundabout and continue on cycle track along riverside under railway.

Pass under two more bridges (one road, one railway). At roundabout by next bridge continue ahead on broad cycle track L of main road. Follow this past football stadium L and bear L past next roundabout. Cross bridge over entrance to Nantes marina and continue on cycle track, bearing L past another roundabout.

Turn R (Quai Magellan) along riverside under Pont Briand bridge, and just after next roundabout follow cycle track turning R across main road. Turn L on cycle track in middle of dual carriageway and continue up ramp to reach N end of Pont Général Audibert bridge in **Nantes** (39km, 7m) (accommodation, refreshments, camping, tourist office, cycle shop, station).

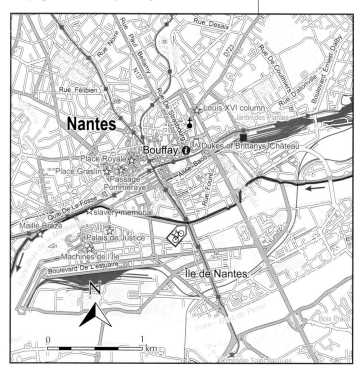

219

NANTES

The eighth largest French city, Nantes (urban pop 655,000) grew up around the confluence of rivers Erdre and Loire and now occupies both banks of the Loire and an island between two arms of the river. Flooding was frequent until it was ended by 20th-century hydrological works. The city centre is on the north bank. Originally a Roman settlement, it became part of the Frankish kingdom after the Romans left. However, its position between the Franks and Bretons led to frequent disputes and in AD851 it became part of Brittany, not returning to French control until 1488. During the Wars of Religion, Nantes was a Catholic stronghold – even though the Edict of Nantes (1598), which guaranteed rights of Protestants, was promulgated in the city. In the early 18th century Nantes became the principal port of western France and a key part of the triangular trade that took manufactured goods to Africa and slaves to the Americas then brought sugar, tobacco and cotton back to Europe. It is estimated that between 1707 and 1831, when the slave trade ended, 550,000 slaves were transported in ships from Nantes. This trade brought huge prosperity to the city and many grand buildings date from this period. Economic development continued through the 19th century with the growth of food production, sugar refining, textile mills and tobacco, fertiliser and armament production, later joined by shipbuilding and in the 20th century aircraft manufacture. In

The Great Elephant is one of the rides in Nantes 'Machines de l'île' theme park

Louis XVI column in Nantes

recent years much of the industry in the inner city has closed, and ex-industrial areas like Île de Nantes are undergoing major redevelopment.

Main tourist sights include the Castle of the Dukes of Brittany, the medieval Bouffay district, the Cathedral of St Peter and St Paul (built 1434–1891), Louis XVI column in Pl Maréchal Foch, the theatre in Pl Graslin, and fountains in Pl Royale that represent the Loire and its tributaries. The indoor Passage Pommeraye shopping arcade (1841) is built over three floors, while the modern 144m Tour Bretagne dominates the skyline. The Brasserie Cigale (1895) in Pl Graslin is decorated in art nouveau style, while the CGA insurance building (1932) is an example of art deco. Recent additions to the city include the new Palais de Justice on Île de Nantes (2000) and a memorial to the abolition of slavery (2012) built into the quayside from where slaving ships departed for Africa. The 'Machines de l'île' theme park is based around mythical beasts and machines found in the novels of Jules Verne, who was born and brought-up in Nantes.

STAGE 26
Nantes to St Brevin-les-Pins (St Nazaire)

Start	Nantes, Général Audibert bridge (7m)
Finish	St Brevin-les-Pins, Mindin maritime museum (4m)
Distance	55km (plus 9.5km to St Nazaire station)
Waymarking	Loire à Vélo (provisional route Nantes–Basse-Indre)

After following the Loire out of Nantes urban area, this long but generally level stage crosses to the south of the river and uses country lanes, canal towpaths and riverside cycle tracks to reach the resort town of St Brevin-les-Pins at the mouth of the Loire. From here a bridge or bus that carries cycles can be used to reach the station in the shipbuilding city of St Nazaire.

From N end of Pont Général Audibert bridge in **Nantes**, cycle W on Quai Moncousu, passing children's hospital R. Go ahead over crossroads at entrance to next bridge and after 50m turn L across road to continue along cycle track L of road (Quai de Tourville). Just before next round-about turn L and R to follow cycle track along riverbank beside Rue Gaston Michel.

Maillé-Brézé is a destroyer built in 1957 and decommissioned as a museum ship in 1988.

Pass pedestrian/cycle bridge with view of ultra-modern Palais de Justice courthouse across river L and continue along riverside cycle track, passing memorial commemorating abolition of the slave trade. Continue past next bridge and pass preserved French naval vessel Maillé-Brézé. ◄

Immediately before Gare Maritime, turn R between car parks to cross main road and turn L on Quai Ernest Renaud (cycle lane R). Pass under bridge linking quay-side with buildings of Gare Maritime passenger terminal, nowadays used by Loire riverbus service. Bear L (do not go uphill) and continue along Bvd de Cardiff to reach round-about. Turn L (sp Indre, third exit, cycle lane R) and bear R along Rue Jules Launey past **Chantenay** station R (4km, 6m) (accommodation, refreshments, cycle shop, station).

Continue along Rue des Usines with railway yards R and industrial area L. Go over railway crossing then follow cycle track across road and pass under motorway bridge to reach roundabout. Pass roundabout R, then follow cycle track back across road and turn L beside Quai Emile Cormerais (sp Indre) through industrial area of St Herblain. At next roundabout turn L (fourth exit, sp Indre–Haute Indre), continuing past industrial buildings L. Continue ahead over next roundabout (sp Indre–Basse-Indre), then fork L onto cycle track after 50m.

Continue through car park and along Esplanade Alphonse Guihut behind houses with garages R and flood meadows L. Where this ends, continue ahead through stone barrier then go up short flight of steps and turn L onto Rue Joseph Tahet. ▶ At next roundabout turn L (Rue Elsa Triolet, third exit, sp Indre–Basse-Indre) and continue over bridge to T-junction. Turn L (Rue du Pont Allard, D75, sp La Montagne), then follow road (Quai Henri Brunais) bearing R beside Loire. After 750m turn L to reach ferry ramp in **Basse-Indre** (10.5km, 5m) (accommodation, refreshments, station). ▶

The steps have wooden fillets to smooth the way for cyclists.

The ferry between Basse-Indre and Indret runs every 15 minutes from 0530 to 2230.

Fishing huts which line the Loire estuary are used to catch flounder

INDRE

The small industrial town of Indre (pop 4000) stands on three former islands in the Loire that rise above the surrounding floodplain. Since the river was straightened and constrained behind flood dykes, Basse-Indre and Haute Indre now lie north of the river while Indret lies to the south. All three originally held fishing villages specialising in catching elver (small eels).

The medieval Mercœur castle on Indret Island was surrounded in 1777 by a huge imperial arsenal built to cast cannons for the French navy. This still stands, now operating as part of DCNS, a major French defence contractor producing maritime propulsion systems. Many of the old arsenal buildings have been preserved and converted into small industrial units.

Metallurgical industry also dominates Basse-Indre where the former Carnaud tinplate rolling mills, which produce cans for the packaging industry, are now operated by Arcelor-Mittal.

Cross river by ferry to Indret and continue away from river (Rue du Bac, D358) on cycle lane R, bearing R to pass **Indret arsenal** R. Continue to reach beginning of Boiseau and turn sharply R (Rue de la Cale), passing below **Boiseau** (12.5km, 5m).

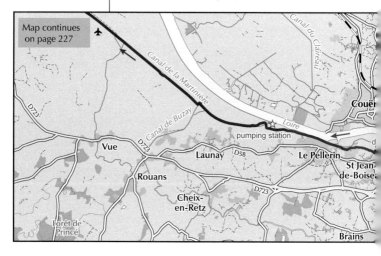

Map continues on page 227

Continue below escarpment that was originally S bank of Loire. Where road bears L uphill, bear R on gravel track and follow this, bearing L into woods. Continue winding through woodland, eventually bearing L, then steeply uphill for a short distance. Emerge onto road (Ch de la Higonnière) and turn R at T-junction (Rue Jean de Martel) into La Noé.

Bear R downhill and take second turn L (Rue des Noëlles du Pé), continuing downhill. Opposite new housing development L, turn R on cycle track through fields. Just before first houses of **St Jean-du-Boiseau**, follow track bearing R, then turn sharply L through gates into Parc Communal du Pé.

Follow unsurfaced track into woodland then turn L over small bridge along L side of grassy area with **Château du Pé** across lake R. Follow track curving R around park to reach T-junction. Bear R on road downhill and bear R again at bottom of hill. Turn immediately L through gap in wall, leaving Parc Communal. Cross next road junction, going ahead L into Rue du Pré Varades. Turn sharply R then bear R on cycle track (Promenade de St Jean-de-Boiseau) through trees for 800m.

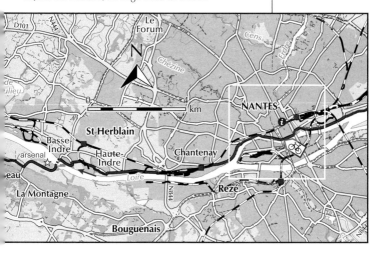

Emerge onto road in La Télindière (17km, 14m) (accommodation) and bear L uphill for short distance. Turn R (Rue du Port), then bear R at T-junction (Rue Abbé Henri Garnier) to reach roundabout with bush in middle. Turn R (Rue du Bac) downhill and continue through open country to reach roundabout at beginning of **Le Pellerin** (18km, 4m) (accommodation, refreshments).

Go ahead through village on Quai du Dr André Provost, passing ferry ramp R, and continue alongside river on Quai des Coteaux. Fork L past shipyard of Les Ateliers des Coteaux R, and where road ends continue ahead (Ch de la Martinière) through barrier onto cycle track through trees parallel with Loire R.

Emerge onto road (Rue de la Tour) and continue ahead (Rue du Canal). Bear R past **pumping station** R and cross bridge over drainage canal. Continue over disused lock R at entrance to **Canal de la Martinière**.

The 15km Canal de la Martinière **ship canal** was dug between 1882–1892 using machinery previously used on the Suez canal. It was designed to

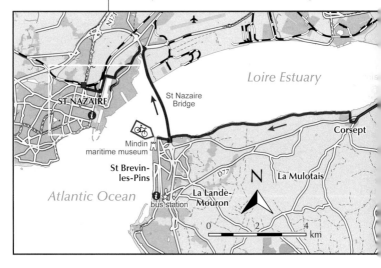

allow large ships to bypass silting problems in the Loire estuary and reach Nantes. After initial success, passages declined as ships grew ever larger and the canal closed in 1959. It now serves as both a hydrological control channel regulating the water level of nearby low-lying marshland and a leisure venue for canoeing, boating and fishing.

Follow road bearing L along canal bank (refreshments) to reach road junction. Dog-leg R and L on road over sluice gates then turn immediately L across canal and R along opposite bank. Continue for 5.5km, passing **Frossay airfield** L, to reach **Le Migron** (32.5km, 2m) (refreshments, camping).

Pass canoe centre and fork R to continue beside canal for another 3km, then turn L at T-junction. Turn R at crossroads and follow quiet country road past **Château du Plessis-Mareil** L. Continue winding through fields for 4km, forking R in Chalopin then crossing wide road and forking R again to reach **La Foucauderie** (40km, 6m) (accommodation). ▶

The wide road crossed before La Foucauderie was built to serve a planned nuclear power station beside the Loire. Although the site was prepared, the project was abandoned unbuilt in 1997.

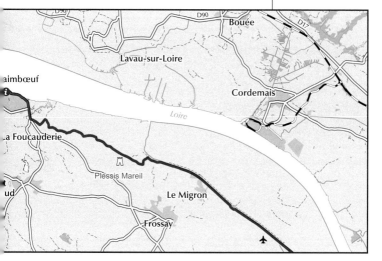

227

The industrial estate is on the site of a former First World War airfield built in 1917 to service American airships hunting German submarines in the Atlantic.

Continue through hamlet to reach T-junction and turn R (Rte de la Virée Longue). Pass industrial estate L and turn L at next T-junction (Rue du Camp d'Aviation). ◄ Turn R at crossroads (Rue du Capitaine Paul Leroy), and where road ends at turning circle continue ahead on gravel track. Emerge onto main road (D723) and turn R on cycle track R. Go ahead at roundabout with model of lighthouse in middle and continue alongside Loire on Quai Edmond Libert. Where road ahead becomes no-entry, turn R and L (Pl Frégate Aréthuse, sp Centre Ville) then immediately R on concrete track along quayside in **Paimbœuf** (43km, 4m) (accommodation, refreshments, camping, tourist office, cycle shop).

> From the mid-17th century **Paimbœuf** (current pop 3000) developed as an important port and shipbuilding centre which grew to service larger vessels unable to navigate the Loire up to Nantes. However, when a decision was taken in the mid-19th century to develop St Nazaire as a major Atlantic port, decline set in and the town is now a sleepy shadow of its former self.

Re-join road and continue beside river on Quai Boulay-Paty. Pass lighthouse R and continue ahead on dual carriageway (Quai Mathurin Gautreau, becoming Quai Éole). Go ahead at mini-roundabout (Rue des Cordiers) past campsite R, then after second roundabout cross road and continue ahead (D77, sp Corsept) using cycle track L. Fork L (Rue de la Mairie, sp St Père-en-Retz) into **Corsept** (45.5km, 5m) (refreshments).

Pass church L and follow road, bearing R (Rue de l'Estuaire). Fork R and continue past cemetery R. Turn R beside car park R, then at end of car park turn R and L onto cycle track. Follow this across road passing round-about L and turn R at second exit (Rue de la Maison-Verte). Fork R beside sluice and follow gravel cycle track bearing L below Loire flood dyke. Continue for 5.5km, then dog-leg L and R beside Metalu factory. Fork R to continue beside Loire then turn sharply R opposite

St Nazaire bridge is the last crossing of the Loire

Gypsy caravan site onto gravel track. ▶ Follow this, bearing L beside estuary and passing hospital L with view of **Pont de St Nazaire** bridge ahead. Where this ends, bear L and continue on road (Ave de Nantes) to reach T-junction.

Turn R (Ave Bordon), passing under road bridge. Turn R opposite house 36 (Ave de la Brière) to reach riverbank. ▶ Turn L beside river (Allée de la Loire) and pass marine navigation tower R to reach end of route by Mindin maritime museum in Pl Bougainville, **St Brevin-les-Pins** (55km, 4m) (accommodation, refreshments, camping, tourist office, cycle shop). You have reached journey's end – well done! Treat yourself to a celebratory drink in the Débarcadère bar and take a picture of Loire à Vélo/EV6 zero km board in Pl Bougainville.

> **St Brevin-les-Pins** (pop 14,000) is a resort town that spreads along the dunes south of the Loire's mouth. Originally a small fishing community, the Mindin headland opposite St Nazaire was fortified by the French military engineer Vauban in 1696. These fortifications now house a maritime museum where

The piers and wooden fishing huts with large nets that line the estuary are used to catch *carrelet* (flounder)

This turn is easy to miss.

the cycle route ends. A project in 1860 to stabilise the dunes by planting pines led to the development of housing and resort facilities including a casino. The opening of the St Nazaire Bridge in 1975 led to greater integration with the industrial economy of St Nazaire. Originally a toll bridge, it became toll-free in 1994, since when there has been a rapid increase in population from 9000 to 14,000.

Public transport to St Nazaire station

Although the cycle route finishes at St Brevin-les-Pins on S side of Loire estuary, this is not a convenient end-point for most cyclists. The nearest station is in St Nazaire, over 9km away by cycle across the St Nazaire Bridge. While the bridge has cycle lanes in both directions, these are narrow and traffic passes by at 100kph. Moreover, there is a steep ascent onto the bridge and if there are side winds this becomes a challenging ride.

There is a bus from St Brevin-les-Pins to St Nazaire station (Aléop, route 317) that takes up to eight cycles per journey, enabling cyclists to avoid riding over the bridge. There are eight services per day Monday–Saturday (three morning rush-hour, two lunchtime, three afternoon rush-hour), with three on Sunday (morning, lunchtime, afternoon). Booking is recommended on tel +33 9 69 39 40 44 between 0800 and 1900 (Monday–Friday), or 0800 and 1200 (Saturday). Buses depart from Pôle de Bresse bus station in centre of St Brevin-les-Pins, 2.5km S of Mindin. Details at www.aleop.paysdelaloire.fr.

Cycle route to St Nazaire station

If you do decide to cycle over the bridge, retrace your route to road bridge. Pass under bridge and turn immediately L on cycle track rising up onto **St Nazaire Bridge**. Cross 3.3km-long cable-stayed bridge on narrow cycle lane R. At bridge end follow slip road bearing R (D100, sp Port de St Nazaire) to reach roundabout. Turn L (sixth exit, sp Port de St Nazaire) and continue under road bridge to second roundabout. Turn R (first exit, Bvd des Apprentis) and cross bridge over river Brivet. Go ahead over two painted roundabouts, passing STX **shipyard** (formerly Chantiers de l'Atlantique) L, then bear R at third roundabout (Ave de Penhoët, second exit, sp St Nazaire centre). Turn L at T-junction (Bvd Paul Leferme) using cycle track R, then turn R at traffic lights (Rue de la Ville-Halluard). Continue over mini-roundabout to reach **St Nazaire station** R (9.5km, 7m) (accommodation, refreshments, tourist office, cycle shop, station).

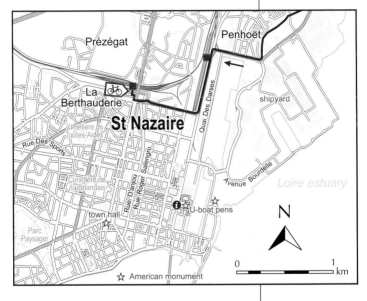

ST NAZAIRE

Before the mid-19th century, St Nazaire (urban pop 153,000) was a small riverside village of fishermen and pilots who took ocean-going ships upriver to Nantes and Paimbœuf. As vessels grew larger and the river silted-up it became difficult for them to negotiate the Loire passage, and in 1850 the French government decided to develop a new port at St Nazaire. This has grown into a major seaport and shipbuilding centre. The shipyards of Chantiers de l'Atlantique built transatlantic liners like Normandie and La

The shipyards in St Nazaire build many of the world's largest cruise ships

France, and more recently Queen Mary II. During the Second World War the port came under Nazi German control. The Joubert dry-dock, the largest on the Atlantic coast, became the home port for German battleships Bismarck and Prince Eugen, but it was destroyed in a raid by British commandos in 1942. On the site of the transatlantic ocean terminal, the Germans constructed a concrete bunker to house 14 U-boat submarine pens. This is 300m long by 130m wide and has a bombproof roof made of 8m-thick concrete and steel. Despite many Allied air raids, which destroyed 98 per cent of the city, the pens survived and are still standing as it has proved too costly to demolish them.

The war lasted nine months longer in St Nazaire and St Brevin than in the rest of France. This was because after the liberation of France in August 1944, the Germans refused to surrender their U-boat facilities in St Nazaire and held onto an area known as the 'St Nazaire pocket' until May 1945. Post-war, the city was rebuilt in minimalist style.

APPENDIX A

Facilities summary

	Distance (km)	Cumulative distance (km)	Altitude (m)	Accommodation	Food	YH (y)/gîte (g)	Camping	Tourist office	Cycle shop	Station
Prologue										
From Le Cheylard										
Le Cheylard			442	x	x	g	x	x		
St Martin-de-Valamas	8	8	551	x	x		x	x		
Arcens	6.5	14.5	626	x	x		x			
St Martial	7	21.5	885		x		x			
La Chaumette				x						
Gerbier de Jonc	10	31.5	1409	x	x	g				
From Langogne										
Langogne			914	x	x		x	x		x
Pradelles	7	7	1159	x	x		x			
Coucouron	12	19	1165	x	x		x			
Lac-d'Issarlès	11	30	935	x	x	g	x	x		
Le Béage	8.5	38.5	1220	x	x	g				
Gerbier de Jonc	12	50.5	1409	x	x	g				
Stage 1										
Ste Eulalie	5.5	5.5	1232	x	x	g	x	x		
Rieutord	7	12.5	1126		x		x			
Lac-d'Issarlès	15.5	28	1001	x	x	g	x	x		
Issarlès	6	34	946	x	x		x			
Goudet	16	50	772	x	x	g	x			
Stage 2										
Ussel	4	54	1027		x	g				
Le Brignon	6.5	60.5	953		x					
Solignac-sur-Loire	6	66.5	856		x					

	Distance (km)	Cumulative distance (km)	Altitude (m)	Accommodation	Food	YH (y)/gîte (g)	Camping	Tourist office	Cycle shop	Station
Brives-Charensac	15	81.5	616	x	x		x			
Le Puy-en-Velay	1.5	83	632	x	x	y/g	x	x	x	x
Stage 3										
Lavoûte-sur-Loire	13	96	562		x		x			x
St Vincent	4	100	550	x						x
Vorey-sur-Arzon	5.5	105.5	541	x	x	g	x	x		x
Le Chambon	4	109.5	551		x		x			
Chamalières-sur-Loire	4.5	114	532		x		x			x
Retournaguet					x					
Retournac	6	120	542	x	x			x		x
Stage 4										
Beauzac	11	131	555		x			x		
La Roche					x					
Bas-en-Basset	6	137	462	x	x	g	x	x		x
Aurec-sur-Loire	13	150	429	x	x	g	x	x		x
Stage 5										
Semène					x					
Le Pertuiset	7.5	157.5	436	x	x	g	x			
Vareilles	2.5	160	522		x					
Chambles	4.5	164.5	635		x	g				
Cessieux	4	168.5	487		x					
St Just-St Rambert	4	172.5	390		x			x		
Bonson				x	x					x
St Cyprien	5	177.5	373		x					
La Rive				x						
Veauchette	4	181.5	356		x					
Rivas	3.5	185	351		x					
Cuzieu	3.5	188.5	350		x					

	Distance (km)	Cumulative distance (km)	Altitude (m)	Accommodation	Food	YH (y)/gîte (g)	Camping	Tourist office	Cycle shop	Station
Meylieu					x					
Montrond-les-Bains	5.5	194	349	x	x			x		x
Feurs	14.5	208.5	346	x	x		x	x	x	x
Stage 6										
Pouilly-lès-Feurs	6.5	215	365		x					
Balbigny	5	220	335		x					x
Lachat				x						
Bernand					x					
Pralery							x			
Pinay	10.5	230.5	410		x					
St Jodard	1.5	232	419		x					x
Château de la Roche	4	236	333		x					
Port de Bully	9	245	333		x					
Bully	3.5	248.5	461		x					
St Jean-St Maurice-s/ Loire	8.5	257	377	x	x					
Les Hauts de Roy					x					
Villerest	7	264	354	x	x		x			
Roanne	7	271	275	x	x			x	x	x
Stage 7										
Briennon	15	286	260	x	x					
Pouilly-sous-Charlieu	1.5	287.5	263	x	x		x			
Iguerande	7	294.5	260	x	x					
Marcigny	9.5	304	249	x	x			x	x	
Baugy					x					
St Yan	16	320	240		x					
Varenne-St Germain	1.5	321.5	240	x						
Digoin	7.5	329	239	x	x		x	x		x

	Distance (km)	Cumulative distance (km)	Altitude (m)	Accommodation	Food	YH (y)/gite (g)	Camping	Tourist office	Cycle shop	Station
Stage 8										
Coulanges	10	339	228		x					
Pierrefitte-sur-Loire	4.5	343.5	226	x	x		x			
Diou				x	x		x			
Bourbon- Lancy	16.5	360	227	x	x		x	x	x	
Stage 9										
Cronat	16	376	228	x	x					
Gannay	3			x	x	g	x			
Charrin	9.5	388.5	197	x	x					
Devay	7.5	396	235	x	x					
Decize	10	406	195	x	x	g	x	x		x
Stage 10										
Fleury-sur-Loire	14	420	184		x					
Chevenon	13	433	178		x		x			
Nevers	7	440	176	x	x		x	x	x	x
Stage 11										
Plagny	2	442	177		x					
Challuy				x						
Gimouille	6.5	448.5	180		x					
Le Guétin	2	450.5	172	x	x					
Le Bec d'Allier					x					
Givry	9	459.5	166		x					
Fourchambault				x	x		x			x
Le Poids-de-Fer					x					
Marseilles-lès-Aubigny	8	467.5	165	x	x					
La Chapelle-Montlinard	12.5	480	156	x	x					
La Charité-sur-Loire				x	x	g	x	x		x

	Distance (km)	Cumulative distance (km)	Altitude (m)	Accommodation	Food	YH (y)/gîte (g)	Camping	Tourist office	Cycle shop	Station
Stage 12										
Pouilly-sur-Loire	13	493	152	x	x		x	x		x
Ménétréol-sous-Sancerre	(10)	503	150	x	x					
Sancerre	(3.5)	506.5	274	x	x			x		
St Thibault	14	504	147	x	x			x		
Stage 13										
St Satur				x	x		x			
Bannay	6	510	149	x	x					
Cosne-Cours-sur-Loire				x	x		x	x		
Belleville-sur-Loire	18	528	139	x	x		x	x		
Beaulieu-sur-Loire	5	533	138	x	x			x		
Mantelot lock (Châtillon)	8	541	129	x	x			x		
Combles lock				x	x		x			
Briare	6	547	134	x	x		x	x		x
Stage 14										
St Brisson-sur-Loire	5.5	552.5	153	x	x					
St Martin-sur-Ocre	2.5	555	137		x					
Gien	4.5	559.5	123	x	x		x	x		x
St Gondon	7	556.5	131	x	x					
St Florent	5.5	572	144	x	x					
Lion-en-Sullias	4.5	576.5	125	x						
Gorgeats					x					
Sully-sur-Loire	11	587.5	111	x	x			x		
Stage 15										
Les Places	4.5	592	112	x						
St Benoît-sur-Loire	3.5	595.5	111	x	x		x	x		

	Distance (km)	Cumulative distance (km)	Altitude (m)	Accommodation	Food	YH (y)/gîte (g)	Camping	Tourist office	Cycle shop	Station
Châteauneuf-sur-Loire	11	606.5	107	x	x		x	x	x	
Jargeau	9.5	616	103	x	x	g	x	x		
Sandillon	7	623	95	x	x					
Orléans	15	638	99	x	x	y	x	x	x	x
Stage 16										
St Hilaire-St Mesmin	7.5	645.5	100	x	x					
Meung-sur-Loire	12.5	658	90	x	x			x		x
Beaugency	8	666	89	x	x		x	x	x	x
Stage 17										
Tavers				x	x					
Avaray					x					
Muides-sur-Loire	17	683	80		x		x			
St Dyé-sur-Loire	(4)	687	88	x	x					
Château de Chambord	(6)	703	79		x					
La Chaussée le Comte	(3.5)	706.5	80	x	x		x			
Huisseau-sur-Cosson	(3.5)	710	79		x		x			
Vineuil	(8)	718	83	x	x					
Blois	17.5	700.5	72	x	x	y/g		x		x
Stage 18										
Chailles	6.5	707	68		x					
Candé-sur-Beuvron	8	715	68	x	x		x			
Chaumont-sur-Loire	6	721	63	x	x		x	x		
Rilly-sur-Loire	4.5	725.5	65	x						
Mosnes	4.5	730	67	x	x		x			
Le Grand Village	2	732	109	x						
Artigny	3	735	105	x						
Amboise	7.5	742.5	59	x	x	g	x	x	x	x

	Distance (km)	Cumulative distance (km)	Altitude (m)	Accommodation	Food	YH (y)/gîte (g)	Camping	Tourist office	Cycle shop	Station
Stage 19										
Lussault-sur-Loire	5.5	748	59		x					
Husseau	4	752	86	x						
Montlouis-sur-Loire	5.5	757.5	73	x	x		x	x		x
Tours	12	769.5	58	x	x			x	x	x
Stage 20										
Joué-lès-Tours	7	776.5	47	x			x			
Le Grand Moulin	5.5	782	45		x					
La Grange	3.5	785.5	45	x						
Savonnières	2.5	788	43	x	x		x			x
Villandry	2.5	790.5	42	x	x			x		
La Chapelle-aux-Naux	8	798.5	39	x						
Bréhémont	6	804.5	38	x	x	g	x		x	
Stage 21										
Rupuanne	3.5	808	38	x						
Rigny-Ussé	3	811	37	x	x		x			
Le Néman	7	818	36	x						
Avoine	4.5	822.5	35	x	x					
Savigny-en-Véron	3.5	826	33	x	x		x			
Candes-St Martin	9.5	835.5	35	x	x	g	x			
Montsoreau	1	836.5	32	x	x		x			
Turquant	3.5	840	39	x	x					
Parnay				x	x					
Dampierre-sur-Loire				x	x					
Saumur	12	852	37	x	x	g	x	x	x	x
Stage 22										
St Hilaire-St Florent	3	855	38	x	x		x			
La Mimerolle	6.5	861.5	28				x			

	Distance (km)	Cumulative distance (km)	Altitude (m)	Accommodation	Food	YH (y)/gîte (g)	Camping	Tourist office	Cycle shop	Station
Chênehutte	1	862.5	31	x	x					
Préban				x	x					
Trèves	3.5	866	26			g				
Cunault	1	867	30	x	x					
Gennes	5	872	30	x	x		x			
Bessé	2.5	874.5	28	x	x					
Le Thoureil	2	876.5	29	x	x					
St Maur	2.5	879	26	x	x					
St Rémy-la-Varenne	3	882	29	x	x	g				
St Mathurin-sur-Loire	1.5	883.5	26	x	x		x	x		x
La Bohalle	6	889.5	19	x						x
La Daguenière	5	894.5	22	x	x					
Angers	(15.5)		38	x	x	y/g	x	x	x	x
Les Ponts-de-Cé	7.5	902	20	x	x		x		x	
Stage 23										
Ste Gemmes-sur-Loire	2.5	904.5	22				x			
Bouchemaine	4.5	909	20	x	x		x		x	
La Pointe	2	911	25	x	x					
Épiré	1.5	912.5	50	x	x					
Savennières	4	916.5	25	x	x					x
La Possonnière	3	919.5	29	x	x		x			x
Le Port Girault	5	924.5	14	x						
Chalonnes-sur-Loire	4.5	929	14	x	x	g			x	x
La Basse Île	4.5	933.5	13		x					
Montjean-sur-Loire	5	938.5	12	x	x		x	x		
Stage 24										
Le Port de Ingrandes	4.5	943	13	x	x		x			x
St Florent-le-Vieil	8.5	951.5	15	x	x		x	x		x

	Distance (km)	Cumulative distance (km)	Altitude (m)	Accommodation	Food	YH (y)/gîte (g)	Camping	Tourist office	Cycle shop	Station
La Fossé Neuf	10	961.5	8	x		g				
Le Fourneau	5	966.5	11		x					
Ancenis	0.5	967	13	x	x		x	x		x
Stage 25										
Oudon	9	976	10	x	x		x	x		x
La Bridonnière								x		
La Varenne	6.5	982.5	10				x			
L'Aireau				x	x					
St Simon La Pinsonnière	6	988.5	8		x					
Mauves-sur-Loire	1.5	990	5	x	x				x	x
Thouaré-sur-Loire	5	995	5	x	x				x	x
Belle Rivière							x			
Bellevue	4	999	5	x	x					
Nantes	7	1006	7	x	x		x	x	x	x
Stage 26										
Chantenay	4	1010	6	x	x				x	x
Basse-Indre	6.5	1016.5	5	x	x					x
La Télindière	6.5	1023	14	x						
Le Pellerin	1	1024	4	x	x					
Canal de la Martinière					x					
Le Migron	14.5	1038.5	2		x		x			
La Foucauderie	7.5	1046	6	x						
Paimbœuf	3	1049	4	x	x		x	x	x	
Corsept	2.5	1051.5	5		x					
St Brevin-les-Pins	9.5	1061	4	x	x		x	x	x	
St Nazaire	9.5		7	x	x			x	x	x

APPENDIX B
Tourist information offices

Le Cheylard
4b Rue St Joseph, 07160
tel +33 4 75 64 80 97
www.ardeche-hautes-vallees.fr

St Martin-de-Valamas
420 Rue du Pont, 07310
tel +33 4 75 64 80 97
www.ardeche-hautes-vallees.fr

Langogne
15 Bvd des Capucins, 48300
tel +33 4 66 69 01 38
www.ot-langogne.com

Stage 1

Ste Eulalie
Le Village, 07510
tel +33 4 75 38 89 78
www.montagnedardeche.com

Lac-d'Issarlès)
Pl de l'Église, 07470
tel +33 4 66 46 86 35
www.montagnedardeche.com
(Jul/Aug only)

Stage 2

Le Puy-en-Velay
2 Pl du Clauzel, 43000
tel +33 4 71 09 38 41
www.lepuyenvelay-tourisme.fr

Stage 3

Vorey-sur-Arzon
L'Embarcadère
Rue Louis Jouvet, 43800
tel +33 4 71 01 30 67
www.lepuyenvelay-tourisme.fr

Retournac
Pl Boncompain, 43130
tel +33 4 71 65 20 50
www.office-de-tourisme-des-sucs-aux-bords-de-loire.fr

Stage 4

Beauzac
13 Rue des Remparts, 43590
tel +33 4 71 61 50 74
www.tourisme-marchesduvelayrochebaron.fr

Bas-en-Basset
16 Boulevard de la Sablière, 43210
tel +33 4 71 66 95 44
www.tourisme-marchesduvelayrochebaron.fr

Aurec-sur-Loire
12 Rue du Commerce, 43310
tel +33 4 77 35 42 65
www.otloiresemene.fr

Stage 5

St Just-St Rambert
7 Pl de la Paix, 42170
tel +33 4 77 96 08 69
www.loireforez.com

Montrond-les-Bains
125 Ave des Sources, 42210
tel +33 4 77 94 64 74
www.forez-est.com

Feurs
Pl Antoine Drivet, 42110
tel +33 4 77 26 05 27
www.forez-est.com

Stage 6

Roanne
8 Pl du Marechal de Lattre
de Tassigny, 42300
tel +33 4 77 71 51 77
www.leroannais.com

Stage 7

Marcigny
Pl des Halles, 71110
tel +33 3 85 25 39 06
www.brionnais-tourisme.fr

Digoin
7 Rue Nationale, 71160
tel +33 3 85 53 00 81
https://tourisme.legrandcharolais.fr

Stage 8

Bourbon-Lancy
15 Pl de la Mairie, 71140
tel +33 3 85 89 18 27
www.tourisme-bourbonlancy.com

Stage 9

Decize
Pl du Champs de Foire, 58300
tel +33 3 86 25 27 23
www.decize-confluence.fr

Stage 10

Nevers
Ducal Palace
4 Rue Sabatier, 58008
tel +33 3 86 68 46 00
www.nevers-tourisme.com

Stage 11

La Charité-sur-Loire
5 Pl Ste Croix, 58400
tel +33 3 86 70 15 06
www.lacharitesurloire-tourisme.com

Stage 12

Pouilly-sur-Loire
30 Rue Waldeck Rousseau, 58150
tel +33 3 86 24 04 70
www.ot-cosnesurloire.com

Sancerre
Esplanade Porte César, 18300
tel +33 2 48 54 08 21
www.tourisme-sancerre.com

St Thibault
Port de Plaisance, 18300
tel +33 2 48 54 08 21
www.tourisme-sancerre.com

Stage 13

Cosne-Cours-sur-Loire
Palais de Loire
Rue du Général de Gaulle, 58205
tel +33 3 86 28 11 85
www.ot-cosnesurloire.com

Belleville-sur-Loire
Rte de Sancerre, 18240
tel +33 2 48 54 08 21
www.tourisme-sancerre.com

Beaulieu-sur-Loire
Pl d'Armes, 45630
tel +33 2 38 31 24 51
www.terresdeloireetcanaux.com

Châtillon-sur-Loire
31 Rue Martial Vuidet, 45360
tel +33 2 38 31 24 51
www.terresdeloireetcanaux.com

Briare
1 Pl Charles de Gaulle, 45250
tel +33 2 38 31 24 51
www.terresdeloireetcanaux.com

Stage 14

Gien
Pl Jean Jaurès, 45500
tel +33 2 38 67 25 28
www.gien-tourisme.fr

Sully-sur-Loire
Pl Charles de Gaulle, 45600
tel +33 2 38 36 23 70
www.tourisme-valdesully.fr

Stage 15

St Benoît-sur-Loire
55 Rue Orléanaise, 45730
tel +33 2 38 35 79 00
www.tourisme-valdesully.fr

Germigny-des-Prés
6 Rte de St Martin, 45110
tel +33 2 38 58 27 97
www.tourisme-valdesully.fr

Châteauneuf-sur-Loire
3 Pl Aristide Briand, 45110
tel +33 2 38 58 44 79
www.valdeloire-foretdorleans.com

Jargeau
Le Chanterie, Bvd Carnot, 45150
tel +33 2 38 59 83 42
www.valdeloire-foretdorleans.com

Orléans
23 Pl du Martroi, 45000
tel +33 2 38 24 05 05
www.tourisme-orleansmetropole.com

Stage 16

Meung-sur-Loire
1 Rue Emmanuel Troulet, 45130
tel +33 2 38 44 32 28
www.tourisme-terresduvaldeloire.fr

Beaugency
3 Pl du Docteur Hyvernaud, 45190
tel +33 2 38 44 32 38
www.tourisme-terresduvaldeloire.fr

Stage 17

Blois
23 Rue de la Voûte du Château, 41000
tel +33 2 54 90 41 41
www.bloischambord.com

Stage 18

Chaumont-sur-Loire
24 Rue du Maréchal Leclerc, 41150
tel +33 2 54 20 91 73
www.bloischambord.com

Amboise
Quai Général de Gaulle, 37400
tel +33 2 47 57 09 28
www.amboise-valdeloire.com

Stage 19

Montlouis-sur-Loire
4 Rue Abraham Courtemanche, 37270
tel +33 2 47 45 85 10
www.tourisme-montlouis-vouvray.fr

Tours
78 Rue de Bernard Palissy, 37042
tel +33 2 47 70 37 37
www.tours-tourisme.fr

Stage 20

Villandry
11 Rue Principal, 37510
tel +33 2 47 50 12 66
www.tours-tourisme.fr

Stage 21

Saumur
8bis Quai Carnot, 49415
tel +33 2 41 40 20 60
www.ot-saumur.fr

Stage 22

St Mathurin-sur-Loire
20 Levée du Roi René, 49250
tel +33 2 41 57 37 55
www.loire-odyssee.fr

Angers
7 Pl du Président Kennedy, 49100
tel +33 2 41 23 50 00
www.tourisme.destination-angers.com

Stage 23

Montjean-sur-Loire
Pl Constant Lebreton, 49570
tel +33 2 41 39 07 07
www.osezmauges.fr

Stage 24

St Florent-le-Vieil
4 Pl de la Février, 49410
tel +33 2 41 72 62 32
www.osezmauges.fr

Ancenis
103 Rue des Douves, 44150
tel +33 2 40 83 07 44
www.pays-ancenis-tourisme.com

Stage 25

Oudon
11 Rue du Pont Levis, 44521
tel +33 2 40 83 07 44
www.pays-ancenis-tourisme.fr

Nantes
9 Rue des États, 44000
tel +33 2 72 64 04 79
www.nantes-tourisme.com

Stage 26

Paimbœuf
Quai Sadi Carnot, 44560
tel +33 2 40 27 53 82
www.saint-brevin.com

St Brevin-les-Pins
10 Rue de l'Église, 44520
tel +33 2 40 27 24 32
www.saint-brevin.fr

St Nazaire
12 Bvd de la Légion d'Honneur, 44600
tel +33 2 40 22 40 65
www.saint-nazaire-tourisme.com

APPENDIX C
Youth hostels and gîtes d'étape

YOUTH HOSTELS

Stage 2

Le Puy-en-Velay (FUAJ) (50 beds)
Centre Pierre Cardinal
9 Rue Jules-Vallès
43000
tel +33 4 71 05 52 40

Stage 15

Orléans (LFAJ) (60 beds)
2 Rue Winston Churchill
45100
tel +33 2 38 53 60 06

Stage 17

Blois (CRJS/FUAJ) (100 beds)
Rue de la Taille aux Moines
41000
tel +33 2 54 52 20 40

Stage 22

Angers (LFAJ) (200 beds)
3 Rue Darwin
49000
tel +33 2 41 22 61 20

GÎTES D'ÉTAPE

Le Cheylard (12 beds)
Camping Le Cheylard
120 Rte de St Agrève
Le Vialon
07160
tel +33 4 75 29 09 53

Le Béage (17 beds)
Lou Biadge
07630
tel +33 4 75 88 44 73

Stage 1

Gerbier de Jonc (13 beds)
Chantal et Gérard Breysse
Au pied du Mont Gerbier
07510
tel +33 4 75 38 81 51

Ste Eulalie (13 beds)
Les Violettes, 07510
tel +33 4 75 37 63 42

Usclades (near Rieutord) (20 beds)
Arthur Torossian
Le Prétaboire
07510
tel +33 4 75 38 95 98

Lac-d'Issarlès (11 beds)
Maison Kopp
301 Rue du Prieuré
07470
tel +33 6 73 76 52 52

Lac-d'Issarlès (8 beds)
La Belette Joyeuse à la Borie
07470
tel +33 4 66 46 26 50

Goudet (19 beds)
Ferme-auberge du Pipet
43150
tel +33 4 71 57 18 05

Stage 2

Ussel (8 beds)
Gîte le Stevenson
43370
tel +33 4 43 07 69 64

Le Puy-en-Velay (19 beds)
Gites d'etape des Capucins
29 Rue des Capucins
43000
tel +33 4 71 04 28 74

Le Puy-en-Velay (19 beds)
Maison St François
6 Rue St Mayol
43000
tel +33 4 71 05 96 86

Le Puy-en-Velay (100 beds)
Centre d'Accueil St Georges
4 Rue St Georges
43000
tel +33 4 71 09 93 10

Stage 3

Vorey (7 beds)
key from Mairie
Pl de la Mairie
43800
tel +33 4 71 03 40 39

Stage 4

Bas-en-Basset (43 beds)
Maison de Vissaguet
43020
tel +33 4 71 66 72 37

Aurec (120 beds)
2 Ch de la Moure
43110
tel +33 4 77 75 00 75

Stage 5

Le Pertuiset (94 beds)
Rte des Échandes
42240
tel +33 4 77 35 72 13

Chambles (34 beds)
La Marianne, Biesse
42170
tel +33 4 77 52 32 33

Chambles (32 beds)
Notre-Dame-de-Grâce
42170
tel +33 4 77 52 14 27

Stage 9

Gannay-sur-Loire (8 beds)
Domaine du Bourg
4 Ch des Terriens
03230
tel +33 6 64 86 65 89

Decize (15 beds)
Séjour du Port
58300
tel +33 3 73 15 00 00

Stage 11

La Charité-sur-Loire (12 beds)
Làô refuge
12 bis Rue Charles Chevalier
58400
tel +33 6 81 27 16 97

Stage 15

Jargeau (17 beds)
Maison de Loire
24 Bvd Carnot
45150
tel +33 2 38 59 76 60

Stage 17

Blois (120 beds)
Centre International Ethic Etapes
37 Rue Pierre et Marie Curie
41007
tel +33 2 54 52 37 00

Stage 18

Amboise (112 beds)
Centre International Ethic Etapes
1 Rue Commire Île d'Or
37400
tel +33 2 47 30 60 90

Stage 20

Bréhémont (30 beds)
Pl du 8 Mai
37130
tel +33 2 47 96 84 71

Stage 21

Candes-St Martin (12 beds)
La Renaissance
1bis Rue du Bac
37500
tel +33 6 87 51 03 69

Saumur (108 beds)
Centre de Séjour
Rue de Verden
l'Île Offard
49400
tel +33 2 41 40 30 00

Stage 22

Trèves (18 beds)
La Métairie
49350
tel +33 2 41 67 92 43

St Rémy-la-Varenne (31 beds)
La Presbytère
Pl de l'Église
49250
tel +33 2 41 54 31 87

Angers (155 beds)
Ethic Etapes
49 Ave du Lac de Maine
49000
tel +33 2 41 22 32 10

Stage 23

Chalonnes-sur-Loire (40 beds)
Les Goulidons
La Corniche Angevine
49290
tel +33 2 41 78 03 58

Stage 24

La Fosse Neuf (18 beds)
Ferme de la Guichetière
49530
tel +33 2 40 09 61 68

APPENDIX D
Useful contacts

Transport

SNCF (French railways)
tel 0844 848 4064
www.sncf-connect.com

Eurostar
tel 0343 218 6186 (reservations)
or 0344 822 5822 (baggage)
www.eurostar.com

Brittany Ferries
tel 0871 244 0744
www.brittany-ferries.co.uk

Condor Ferries
tel 0845 609 1024
www.condorferries.co.uk

European Bike Express
tel 01430 422111
info@bike-express.co.uk
www.bike-express.co.uk

The man in seat 61
(rail travel information)
www.seat61.com

Excess Baggage Company
(bike boxes at London airports)
www.left-baggage.co.uk

Valence–Le Cheylard buses
Transports Arome/Cars de l'Eyrieux
cycle reservations +33 (0)9 70 82 15 60
www.auvergnerhonealpes.fr/
interurbainardeche

St Brevin–St Nazaire buses, Aléop
cycle reservations +33 (0)9 69 39 40 44
www.aleop.paysdelaloire.fr

Cycling organisations

Cycling UK
(formerly Cyclists' Touring Club)
Parklands, Railton Rd
Guildford GU2 9JX
tel 01483 238301 (membership)
tel 0844 736 8458 (insurance)
www.cyclinguk.org

Maps and guides

La Loire à Vélo route guide
www.loireavelo.fr

EuroVelo EV6 route guide
www.eurovelo.com/ev6/France

Huber Kartographie
www.cartography-huber.com

Open Street Map (online mapping)
www.openstreetmap.org

Stanfords
7 Mercer Walk, London WC2H 9AF
tel 0207 836 1321
sales@stanfords.co.uk
www.stanfords.co.uk

The Map Shop
15 High St, Upton upon Severn,
Worcs WR8 0HJ
tel 0800 085 4080 or 01684 593146
themapshop@btinternet.com
www.themapshop.co.uk

Accommodation

Youth Hostels Association
tel 0800 019 1700
customerservices@yha.org.uk
www.yha.org.uk

Hostelling International
(youth hostel bookings)
www.hihostels.com

Gites d'étape guide
www.gites-refuges.com

APPENDIX E
Language glossary

English	French
yes	*oui*
no	*non*
please	*s'il vous plaît*
thank you	*merci*
abbey	*l'abbaye (f)*
barrier	*la barrière*
bicycle	*le vélo*
brake	*le frein*
bridge	*le pont*
castle	*le château*
cathedral	*la cathédrale*
church	*l'église (f)*
cycle track	*la véloroute*
cyclist	*le cycliste*
dam	*le barrage*
diversion	*le déviation*
dyke	*la levée*
ferry	*le bac*
field	*le champ*
flood	*l'inondation (f)*

English	French
forest/woods	*la forêt/les bois*
fort	*le fort*
lock	*l'écluse (f)*
monastery	*le monastère*
monument	*le monument*
motorway	*l'autoroute (f)*
no entry	*entrée interdite*
one-way street	*sens unique*
puncture	*la crevaison*
railway	*le chemin de fer*
river	*la fleuve*
riverbank	*la rive*
road closed	*route fermée*
station	*la gare*
tourist information office	*la syndicat d'initiative/l'office de tourisme (m)*
town hall/city hall	*la mairie//l'hôtel de ville (f)*
youth hostel	*l'auberge de jeunesse (f)*

NOTES

DOWNLOAD THE ROUTES
IN GPX FORMAT

All the routes in this guide are available for download from:

www.cicerone.co.uk/1083/GPX

as standard format GPX files. You should be able to load them into most online GPX systems and mobile devices, whether GPS or smartphone. You may need to convert the file into your preferred format using a conversion programme such as gpsvisualizer.com or one of the many other such websites and programmes.

When you follow this link, you will be asked for your email address and where you purchased the guidebook, and have the option to subscribe to the Cicerone e-newsletter.

www.cicerone.co.uk

LISTING OF CICERONE GUIDES

Shorter Walks in the Dolomites
Ski Touring and Snowshoeing in
   the Dolomites
The Way of St Francis
Trekking in the Apennines
Trekking in the Dolomites
Trekking the Giants' Trail: Alta Via 1
   through the Italian Pennine Alps
Via Ferratas of the Italian Dolomites
   Vols 1&2
Walking and Trekking in the
   Gran Paradiso
Walking in Abruzzo
Walking in Italy's Cinque Terre
Walking in Italy's Stelvio
   National Park
Walking in Sicily
Walking in the Dolomites
Walking in Tuscany
Walking in Umbria
Walking Lake Como and Maggiore
Walking Lake Garda and Iseo
Walking on the Amalfi Coast
Walking the Via Francigena
   pilgrim route – Parts 2&3
Walks and Treks in the
   Maritime Alps

MEDITERRANEAN
The High Mountains of Crete
Trekking in Greece
Treks and Climbs in Wadi Rum,
   Jordan
Walking and Trekking in Zagori
Walking and Trekking on Corfu
Walking in Cyprus
Walking on Malta
Walking on the Greek Islands –
   the Cyclades

NEW ZEALAND & AUSTRALIA
Hiking the Overland Track

NORTH AMERICA
The John Muir Trail
The Pacific Crest Trail

SOUTH AMERICA
Aconcagua and the Southern Andes
Hiking and Biking Peru's Inca Trails
Torres del Paine

**SCANDINAVIA, ICELAND
AND GREENLAND**
Hiking in Norway – South
Trekking in Greenland – The Arctic
   Circle Trail
Trekking the Kungsleden
Walking and Trekking in Iceland

**SLOVENIA, CROATIA,
MONTENEGRO AND ALBANIA**
Mountain Biking in Slovenia
The Islands of Croatia
The Julian Alps of Slovenia
The Mountains of Montenegro
The Peaks of the Balkans Trail
The Slovene Mountain Trail
Walking in Slovenia: The Karavanke
Walks and Treks in Croatia

SPAIN AND PORTUGAL
Camino de Santiago:
   Camino Frances
Coastal Walks in Andalucia
Cycling the Camino de Santiago
Cycling the Ruta Via de la Plata
Mountain Walking in Mallorca
Mountain Walking in
   Southern Catalunya
Portugal's Rota Vicentina
Spain's Sendero Historico: The GR1
The Andalucian Coast to Coast Walk
The Camino del Norte and
   Camino Primitivo
The Camino Ingles and Ruta do Mar
The Camino Portugues
The Mountains of Nerja
The Mountains of Ronda
   and Grazalema
The Sierras of Extremadura
Trekking in Mallorca
Trekking in the Canary Islands
Trekking the GR7 in Andalucia
Walking and Trekking in the
   Sierra Nevada
Walking in Andalucia
Walking in Menorca
Walking in Portugal
Walking in the Algarve
Walking in the Cordillera Cantabrica
Walking on Gran Canaria
Walking on La Gomera and El Hierro
Walking on La Palma
Walking on Lanzarote
   and Fuerteventura
Walking on Madeira
Walking on Tenerife
Walking on the Azores
Walking on the Costa Blanca
Walking the Camino dos Faros

SWITZERLAND
Switzerland's Jura Crest Trail
The Swiss Alpine Pass Route –
   Via Alpina Route 1
The Swiss Alps
Tour of the Jungfrau Region
Walking in the Bernese Oberland

Walking in the Engadine –
   Switzerland
Walking in the Valais
Walking in Zermatt and Saas-Fee

JAPAN AND ASIA
Hiking and Trekking in the Japan
   Alps and Mount Fuji
Japan's Kumano Kodo Pilgrimage
Trekking in Tajikistan

HIMALAYA
Annapurna
Everest: A Trekker's Guide
Trekking in Bhutan
Trekking in Ladakh
Trekking in the Himalaya

MOUNTAIN LITERATURE
8000 metres
A Walk in the Clouds
Abode of the Gods
Fifty Years of Adventure
The Pennine Way – the Path,
   the People, the Journey
Unjustifiable Risk?

TECHNIQUES
Fastpacking
Geocaching in the UK
Map and Compass
Outdoor Photography
Polar Exploration
The Mountain Hut Book

MINI GUIDES
Alpine Flowers
Navigation
Pocket First Aid and Wilderness
   Medicine
Snow

For full information on all our guides,
books and eBooks,
visit our website:
www.cicerone.co.uk